THE
BLUE JAY'S
DANCE

THE
BLUE JAY'S
DANCE

A Birth Year

LOUISE ERDRICH

HarperCollins*Publishers*

HarperCollins books may be purchased for educational, business, or sales promotional use. For information, please write: Special Markets Department, HarperCollins Publishers, Inc., 10 East 53rd Street, New York, NY 10022.

FIRST EDITION

Designed by Jessica Shatan

LIBRARY OF CONGRESS CATALOGING-IN-PUBLICATION DATA
Erdrich, Louise.
    The blue jay's dance : a birth year / Louise Erdrich. —
1st ed.
        p.   cm.
    ISBN 0-06-017132-4
    1. Erdrich, Louise—Family.   2. Woman novelists, American—20th century—Family relationships.   3. Mothers and daughters—United States.   4. Motherhood.
    5. Childbirth.   I. Title.
    PS3555.R42Z464   1995
    813'.54—dc20
    [B]   94-23768

95 96 97 98 99 ❖/RRD 10 9 8 7 6 5 4 3 2 1

Acknowledgments

Parts of this book have been published in the following magazines. I would like to thank the editors. "Women's Work," in *Harpers*, edited by Ilena Silverman; "Foxglove. Woman of the House," in *Georgia Review*, edited by Stanley Lindberg (part of "Foxglove" was also reprinted in *Harpers*); "Skunk Dreams," in *Georgia Review*, edited by Stanley Lindberg, reprinted in *The Best American Essays, 1994* and also *Pushcart Prize Anthology*, thanks to Michael Martone. "Wintergardens" was published in the anthology *Summer*, edited by Alice Gordon. "Driving Slick Roads" appeared in *Civilization*, edited by Robert Wilson. "Nests" was published in *Ladies' Home Journal* and excerpted for *Reader's Digest*. "The Veils" appeared in the book *Transforming a Rape Culture*, edited by Emilie Buchwald (Milkweed Press).

I would like to especially thank Brenda Wehle for reading and beautifully performing parts of *Harpers*' "Women's Work" and "The Veils." Susan Moldow and Wendy Wolf edited this book at various stages. Sandi Campbell smoothed the way. Donald Hall and Charlotte Houde had enormous patience during difficult times. Michael Dorris believed I could and my mother, Rita Gourneau Erdrich, and my father, Ralph Erdrich, taught me how.

Dedication and Household Map

I finished this book for our daughters because I hope these pages will claim for them and for others, too, what it is to be a parent—an experience shattering, ridiculous, earthbound, deeply warm, rich, profound. The baby described is a combination of our three babies whom I nursed and cared for in a series of writing offices. I do not name our children, and if I refer to them obliquely sometimes, I hope that readers will forgive. After all, these words will one day add to our daughters' memories, which are really theirs alone.

In case the reader becomes confused, I offer here a thumbnail sketch of our household setup. When this book was written, our three youngest daughters were at home—one a baby and two in preschool. We had three older adoptive children—a daughter in high school and two sons, one of whom was learning disabled as the result of Fetal Alcohol Syndrome. My husband, Michael Dorris, wrote in our farmhouse and I in a little rental house across the road. His family is in Kentucky and eastern Washington and mine largely in North Dakota. The farm is in New Hampshire. We had a kind-eyed dog and many cats.

I am not a scientist, not a naturalist, not a chef, not an expert, not the best or worst mother, but a writer only, a woman constantly surprised. Michael not only dealt with the outside world during these enclosed times but opened his life to me. We raised our children as equally as we could, responding to an ever changing and complex variety of ages and needs. He has always bought me time at the expense of his own—and for this I dearly and tenderly thank him.

This book is dedicated to my husband and to our daughters—dear ones, to your true and brave friendship!

You wakened this book in my mind, you gave
       it to me;
for the words I spoke in delight and from a full
       heart
were echoed back from your sweet life.

—MARIANNE VON WILLEMER,
                        adapted by Goethe

PART I

Winter

Making Babies

WE CONCEIVE OUR CHILDREN IN DEEPEST night, in blazing sun, outdoors, in barns and alleys and minivans. We have no rules, no ceremonies, we don't even need a driver's license. Conception is often something of a by-product of sex, a candle in a one-room studio, pure brute chance, a wonder. To make love with the desire for a child is to move the act out of its singularity, to make the need of the moment an eternal wish. But of all passing notions, that of a human being for a child is perhaps the purest in the abstract, and the most complicated in reality. Growing, bearing, mothering or fathering, supporting, and at last letting go of an infant is a powerful and mundane creative act that rapturously sucks up whole chunks of life.

Other parents—among them, the first female judge appointed in New Hampshire, my own mid-wife, a perpetually overwhelmed movie researcher and television producer, and our neighbor, who baby-sits to make a difficult living—seem surprised at their own helplessness in the face of the passion they feel for their children. We live and work with a divided consciousness. It is a beautiful enough shock to fall in love with another adult, to feel the possibility of unbearable sorrow at the loss of that other, essential, personality, expressed just so, that particular touch. But love of an infant is of a different order. It is twinned love, all absorbing, a blur of boundaries and messages. It is uncomfortably close to self-erasure, and in the face of it one's fat ambitions, desperations, private icons, and urges fall away into a dreamlike *before* that haunts and forces itself into the present with tough persistence.

The self will not be forced under, nor will the baby's needs gracefully retreat. The world tips away when we look into our children's faces. The days flood by. Time with children runs through our fingers like water as we lift our hands, try to hold, to capture, to fix moments in a lens, a magic circle of images or words. We snap photos, videotape, memorialize while we experience a fast-forward in which there is no replay of even a single instant.

We have a baby. Our sixth child, our third birth. During that year, our older, adopted children hit adolescence like runaway trucks. Dear grandparents weaken and die. Michael rises at four in the morning, hardly seems to sleep at all. To keep the door to the other self—the writing self—open, I scratch messages on the envelopes of letters I can't answer, in the margins of books I'm too tired to review. On pharmacy prescription bags, dime-store notebooks, children's construction paper, I keep writing.

This book is a set of thoughts from one self to the other—writer to parent, artist to mother. For me, as for many women, work means necessary income. For a writer, work is also emotional and intellectual survival: it is who I am. I don't stop working, and reworking, and publishing fiction. No matter what life throws at me—and I've had far more difficult obstacles than the intense experience of having children—I expect and offer no excuses. That's not at all what this book is about.

These pages are a personal search and an extended wondering at life's complexity. This is a book of conflict, a book of babyhood, a book about luck, cats, a writing life, wild places in the world, and my husband's cooking. It is a book about the vitality between mothers and infants, that passionate and artful bond into which we pour the direct expression of our being.

For men primarily responsible for their baby's care, please accept this book as your own as well, for you are magnificent. Gender correctness aside, historically and most often these days it is a woman who takes on the tender and grueling task of rearing a newborn. Writing is reflective and living is active—the two collide in the tumultuous business of caring for babies. She bathes her children, she mends the torn armholes of favorite shirts, he picks out birthday party gifts, they receive breathtaking confidences. He and she see the next world and the next reflected in the ocean of their newborn's eyes.

December. Deep snow and middle trimester. Where I Work.

THE SMALL GRAY HOUSE WHERE I WORK was built in the hope of feeding snowmobilers. Twenty years ago, a rough trail was carved out of New Hampshire timberland a hundred yards from the door. Buzzing down from the trailhead—hidden now by thick growth of pine and maple—bundled riders were supposed to stop here for hot chocolate, hot dogs, doughnuts drizzled with maple syrup. But the plan fell through before it could be tested, and now, all this long winter, I hear no more than a dozen snowmobilers pass by, though the snowfall is deep. An oddly shaped window in my back room still opens where the counter was supposed to be, but instead of a stove and deep fryer, books line the walls.

In its first years, this place was rented out to a series of people who believed themselves handy with tools, and as a result it is a strange house: constantly improved, but still missing fixtures, light socket covers, cupboard doors. The man who drove a Pepsi delivery truck for a living fit together a wall of bricks behind the small, black woodstove. One renter cultivated a marijuana patch at a secluded edge of our land, put in a carpet, and punched round fist-holes into the Sheetrock one night in a jealous fit. Those who've lived in this house haunt it, and their dogs do too. The brown Doberman, the harlequin Great Dane, and the two willful breedless dogs with wide muzzles, short hair, and horrifying growls have laid out invisible and possibly eternal territories of scent. Our gentle dog, an Australian Shepherd from hard-working parents, leaves me at the door every morning and watches me enter with intelligent, worried eyes. His instinct is to protect, but he finds the welter of old scents confusing. There seems to be no danger, and yet, perhaps . . .

There was also, in this house's short life, a suicide. I don't know much about him except that he was young, lived alone, rode a motorcycle to work. I don't know where in the house he was when he shot himself. I do not want to know, except I do know. There is only one place. It is here, where I sit, before the window, looking out into the dark shapes of trees.

Perhaps it is odd to contemplate a subject grim as suicide while anticipating a child so new she'll wear a navel tassel and smell of nothing but her purest self, but beginnings suggest endings and I can't help thinking about the continuum, the span, the afters, and the befores.

I COME here every day to work, starting while invisibly pregnant. I imagine myself somewhere else, into another skin, another person, another time. Yet simultaneously my body is constructing its own character. It requires no thought at all for me to form and fix a whole other person. First she is nothing, then she is growing and dividing at such a rate I think I'll drop. I come in eager hope and afraid of labor, all at once, for this is the heart of the matter. Whatever else I do, when it comes to pregnancy I am my physical self first, as are all of us women. We can pump gas, lift weights, head a corporation, lead nations, and tune pianos. Still, our bodies are rounded vases of skin and bones and blood that seem impossibly engineered for birth. I look down onto my smooth, huge lap, feel my baby twist, and I can't figure out how I'll ever stretch wide enough. I fear I've made a ship inside a bottle. I'll have to break. I'm not me. I feel myself becoming less a person than a place, inhabited, a foreign land. I will experience pain, lose physical control, or know the uncertainty of anesthetic. I fear these things, but vaguely, for my brain buzzes in the merciful wash of endorphins that preclude any thought from occupying it too long. Most of all, I worry over what I hold. I want perfection. Each day I pray another perfect cell to form. A million of them. I fear that my tears, my moods, my wrenched weeping will imprint on the baby's psyche. I fear repression, a stoic face shown to the world, will cause our child to hide emotions. I make too much of myself, expect too many favors, or not enough. I rock and rock and stare out the window into my life.

Blue Jays

I COME TO THIS LITTLE HOUSE MORNING-sick, then heavier, wearing a path through snow, carrying an orange plastic sand pail full of birdseed. I come here hoping to find a couple of words to rub together. I cast my bread on the waters and feed the ravens, the woodpeckers and the handsome black and yellow evening grosbeaks who land in flocks, and the blue jays.

Nuisance birds, the jays are all screeching greed and hungry jeers. Over the years we've lived here, their numbers have grown from the scruffy two who fed off spilled cat food and nested near the back door to nearly a dozen. I think of them as a bomb squad, a gang, a small platoon. As soon as I've put down the seed, before I've even gone into the little house and closed the door, the jays appear, kamikaze-diving from the low branches of the poplars, plucking themselves upward at the final instant in swift chandelles. They feed voraciously, filling their crops without pausing to remove shells. They zip off to cache their seeds and return with a desperation of intent that would be comical if it weren't for the way they threaten the miniature chickadees, the shy and solitary nuthatches, the purple finches, state birds of New Hampshire—described by Roger Tory Peterson and our five-year-old daughter exactly the same way: sparrows held by the feet and dipped into raspberry juice.

Advice

MOST OF THE INSTRUCTION GIVEN TO PREGnant women is as chirpy and condescending as the usual run of maternity clothes—the wide tops with droopy bows slung beneath the neck, the T-shirts with arrows pointing to what can't be missed, the childish sailor collars, puffed sleeves, and pastels. It is cute advice—what to pack in the hospital bag (don't forget a toothbrush, deodorant, a comb or hair dryer)—or it's worse: pseudo-spiritual, misleading, silly, and even cruel. In giving birth to three daughters, I have found it impossible to eliminate pain through breathing, by focusing on a soothing photograph. It is true *pain* one is attempting to endure in drugless labor, not "discomfort," and the way to deal with pain is not to call it something else but to increase in strength, to prepare the will. Women are strong, strong, terribly strong. We don't know how strong we are until we're pushing out our babies. We are too often treated like babies having babies when we should be in training, like acolytes, novices to high priestesshood, like serious applicants for the space program.

January. Sweet hopes and poker hands.

THE BLUEPRINT FOR ALL OUR INHERITED characteristics is provided by the DNA molecules in the nuclei of our cells. The entire structure is composed of roughly three billion such pairs, together making up 100,000 genes. It is thrilling, dizzying, to consider the order of these pairs in the human genome, the total genetic message. Staring into my lap, I imagine genes shuffling together like poker hands and my thoughts swim toward stacked, incalculable numbers.

When we make love in the darkness of anticipation we are inviting accident and order, the careful lining up of genes. Unlocking the components of another person, we are safecrackers—setting the combinations, unconsciously twirling dials. Shadow brothers, sisters, potential unfused others, cease. Our children grow into existence particularized, yet random.

Eating

IT ISN'T JUST EATING, OF COURSE, AND THERE'S the joy. Now it's even better, for I never know which bite is destined for the heart, the muscles, hair, the bones forming like the stalks of flowers, or the lovely eyes. Michael makes Jell-O for me so that the baby will have perfect fingernails. He attempts, in his cooking, to get every part of the baby right. Of course, the real challenge in the beginning of pregnancy is how to find exactly what food is bearable in the clutch of morning sickness.

Sleep is the only truly palatable food at first. I sleep hungrily, angry, needy for sleep, jealous for sleep, devouring it and yet resentful of the time it takes away from conscious life. I dream crazily, powerfully. I catch touchdown passes for the Vikings, incite the jealousy of Princess Di, talk earnestly and intimately with a huge male Kodiak brown bear, fly headlong over these low northeastern mountains. Morning comes. I throw up quickly, efficiently, miserably, and eat a cracker. It does no good at all to fight the feeling. For garden-variety morning sickness, which is all I've ever had, not the serious kind that requires hospitalization, very little can be done except to endure. I am not an advice giver, but I will offer these helpful strategies. When very sick, plain saltines are the best. They are an everyday cracker, though, and one should watch for sales on expensive English water biscuits—something special for the weekends. Plain low-salt wheat thins, Stoned Wheat Thins, mild Cheddar Goldfish crackers, Bremner Wafers, and an occasional cardboard Finland toast make you feel ascetic, balanced. I eat matzos in great tiles and sheets. A meal of croissant crackers and ginger ale drunk from Michael's grandmother's wineglass is both mournful and restorative. The perfect love-gift for this delicate time? A box of Carr's assorted crackers, all of which come in complex toasted shapes, so that you can pretend you are actually eating a variety of foods.

Around month four, if you are fortunate, when

you can eat any food and have a roaring appetite, try something intense—say, a food associated with a first love affair, provided you regard it now with nostalgic joy and are glad it's finished. A jar of bittersweet chocolate syrup, perhaps, only to be licked from a bare finger. These next few months are the most sensuous and sexual of your life—you're not too big and your baby's not in the way and your breasts are stunning creatures right from the Song of Solomon.

You will need every resource.

Perhaps you didn't eat during your fateful encounters, or cannot remember what, or perhaps your greatest emotions were of the intellect, or perhaps you are a plain eater and never developed the taste for an aphrodisiac before, or you could be having this baby all on your own, for which you should be simply adored. At any rate, just in case, I offer the following possible candidates as the most sensuous of foods—a fresh cold cherry soup made with a little cream and cinnamon. Fry bread cooked small, in new oil, with a dollop of chokecherry jam. Hawaiian kettle-fried potato chips. Flan. Anything barbecued.

I cook day in and day out, more or less following recipes, and I'm quite good at my job—my worst culinary sin, as I am interested in protecting my daughters from hormone-fed meats, is that I often attempt to foist off tofu in experimental disguises. It is Michael who puts his mind wholeheartedly to the task of making meals, takes up the holiday challenge. He is a special-occasions cook, best at creating symbolic feasts. He searches out exotica and wields a stunning array of equipment—choppers, grinders, springform pans—whereas I use nothing more than a well-sharpened knife. Sometimes his style irritates me—I think it is macho cooking, which I must then loudly appreciate—as opposed to my workaday pastas. But no sooner do I think this than a dish he brings forth in the heat of secrecy erases my resentment.

Michael was raised by a mother and two aunts, surrounded by daughters, married to me. I suppose it is no wonder he has collected a great many recipes guaranteed to cool and soothe irascible women. Pregnant or not, I find that I always respond to his extraordinarily tart lemon meringue pie. It is his signature offering, and I'll eat it morning, noon, night. He knows, also, that it produces a general amnesty of tone in me—as if the shocking little bursts of citrus paralyze some critical nerve.

LEMON MERINGUE PIE

1 cup sugar
3 tablespoons flour
3 tablespoons cornstarch
⅛ teaspoon salt
1 ½ cups boiling water
3 egg yolks
2 teaspoons grated lemon rind
⅓ cup fresh lemon juice
2 tablespoons butter
Baked pastry shell for a 9-inch pie

Meringue
4 egg whites
Pinch of cream of tartar
7 tablespoons sugar
1 teaspoon lemon juice

1. Mix half the sugar with the flour, cornstarch, and salt in a 2-quart saucepan or the top of a double boiler. Stir in the boiling water. Cook over low heat, stirring constantly until the mixture begins to boil. Immediately turn the heat low and stir 3 or 4 minutes longer.

2. Beat the remaining sugar into the egg yolks, then slowly stir in some of the hot sugar mixture. When combined, add back into the sugar mixture. Continue to stir and cook for roughly 2 minutes or until the egg is set.

3. Remove from heat and let cool for 2 to 3 minutes. Add the grated lemon rind and juice. Stir in the butter.

4. Set aside the filling while you prepare the meringue. In a large bowl whisk the egg whites until frothy, then add the cream of tartar. Add the sugar 1 tablespoon at a time, until peaks form. Just before the last whip, add the lemon juice.

5. Turn the filling into the pie shell and top with the meringue, spreading it evenly and making sure to cover the rim of the crust. Make peaks with fork tines in pattern.

6. Bake 20 minutes at 300 degrees or until golden brown highlights appear.

TV Dinner

OUR HOUSE HAS NO PUMP, BUT RECEIVES ITS water via gravity from a shallow well uphill which contains, in a wet year, cold, leaf-filtered rainwater that keeps a mineral volume in the mouth, and tastes as though it has run through the roots of birch trees. One morning two pregnancies ago, however, during a drought, I turned the faucet wide and heard the thunk and yawn of air in the pipes. The hollow sound reverberated right through my body, for I knew immediately that the well had gone dry. As we had no money to drill a well, we hauled water for a month, showered in the school gym, and used the thickets and underbrush that stretched for miles around the house.

I don't recommend the experience, but sometimes I think that our baby's emotional wealth and appreciation of the natural world was assisted by the fact that I rose at three each morning to walk out into the night woods. Fireflies throbbed in the heavy blackness, sending out ardent messages. I paused sleepily to watch. Surely our baby heard the thin riffs of crickets that ceased and swelled after my steps, and surely the night oxygen bubbled into her, blood rich, cool, and dark.

The point of describing this aridity, however, is to return to the meal—the enchilada TV dinner. We stocked our freezer with frozen foods because they included their own plastic or foil trays—no dishes to wash. A dry house feels hollow. On entering, the place immediately felt rainless and dirty, ungiving, gritty, unclean, lacking. We had electricity, though, and in the freezer TV dinners.

One evening, I lay on the couch before the television, as if because we were going to eat a TV dinner I should watch TV. An episode of *Family Feud* began and I remember thinking that there was something truly unbearable about what was happening to me: all that college angst, for this! Suddenly, I smelled ersatz Mexican food. At certain times, powdered nacho flavoring has, to me, the manna power to ward off all harms and exhaustions. I often crave fake cheese powder and all its forms and pomps and circumstances, and so when Michael brought me the steaming foil tray with the two enchiladas plumped out, just so, by virtue of his exact timing of the right amount of oven heat, even bearing dabs of new-bought sour cream, flanked by mounds of lard-rich refried beans and onion-pepper rice, I was abjectly grateful. At the same time, I was humbled that I could be brought so low as to feel this was a magic moment. Though still dull, I sat up and put the first forkful into my mouth, and the next, the next. I ate half the enchilada and then began on the rice, which contained a wire.

I chewed the wire. Irritated, I put the wire on my plate and continued to eat the dinner as beside me Michael ate his own identical enchilada TV dinner.

"Hey," I said to him. "Was there a wire in yours?"

That's when I burst into tears—was it because I suddenly knew I couldn't eat the rest of the dinner? Not with a wire in it. Was it because I felt so American—dry, brutally amused by a game show, hungry, with a wire in my food? I cried so pathetically that the sound caused me to laugh—the laughter grew hysterical.

We decided this could be our lucky day—we could sue the TV dinner company for enough money to sink an eight-hundred-foot well! Michael consulted a college friend attorney who inquired whether "the little one" had seen the wire or been traumatized. On his advice, we froze the rest of my dinner then photocopied it the next day in the basement of the library at Dartmouth College. Michael sent the incriminating page, along with a diatribe of professorial outrage, straight to the manufacturer's corporate address. One week later a vice president replied with a letter of cautious regret, admitting to nothing, but including a fifty-dollar gift certificate for, what else, more TV dinners.

Licorice and Metaphysics

I LUMBER UP AND DOWN THESE ROADS hoping to engage my baby's head, hoping she will "drop." With our due date in sight, that is all we talk about—dropping and engaging—so that I picture her as a rocket aimed straight out of me. The last months and weeks of pregnancy are an endless string of hours, the most difficult weeks in which to stay balanced. Time stops and tension builds with every breath. Fear presses its paws on my chest. I am so heavy that just to mention my suffering is not enough—I buy a fifty-pound sack of potatoes. Anyone who doubts my daily effort can lift this sack and understand why I'm not in a good mood. Fifty extra pounds is what I carry with me at all times.

I suppose, to be accurate, it should be fifty pounds of licorice. To quit smoking I took the old family remedy, passed down from my Ojibwa grandfather, Pat Gourneau—black licorice. He gave up snuff for all forms of licorice, the root itself, delicious, splintery, as well as ropes, wheels, pipes, twists. My body is now an awkward old-fashioned fifties-movie diving suit, huge on me, pressurized, made of black licorice. I'm on the bottom of the ocean taking deep, slow breaths that rise over me in visible bubbles.

I walk out onto the trails every day, no matter how grim the weather. After a deep snow, I plow calmly through thigh-high powder. My body's padded, warm and down-packed. I can sit anywhere, for hours. I lounge in the snow to think as the sun drops a feeble and indifferent light. The cold does not penetrate. I roll over, a whale in snow dunes, and lie quietly on my back, wishing I could bear this baby quickly, fervently, right out here in this field, alone.

Hour of the wolf

PART OF A WRITER'S TASK IS TO PUT HER failings at the service of her pen. Just so with insomnia, this habit of waking at the most inconvenient, still hour of what is technically morning—three or four A.M.—the hour of the wolf. My eyes flip open. All the lights are on in my head, thoughts alert and humming. In past times, I could think of the fictional question or problem I was facing, and my brain would snap right off as though confronted by a paralyzing koan. No more. Pregnancy increases my tendency to wakefulness and makes any sleeping medication dangerous, since it passes into the baby affecting god-knows-what developmental moment. As a matter of practicality, knowing I'll be burnt-out and drowsy the next day if I lie stewing and planning in the dark, I get up. I make myself a cup of herbal tea and start writing poetry. The house is bleak and cold, the windows painted with ostrich ferns of frost. I stir the tea, quietly, then swaddle myself in afghans on the living room couch and write until my words lull me back to sleep. Often, satisfactorily weary at four-thirty or five, I pass Michael on the stairs as he rises to stoke the wood fire, make coffee, begin his day.

I write poems during the late nights up until the week of birth, and fiction by day. I suppose one could say, pulling in the obvious metaphors, that my work is hormone driven, inscribed in mother's milk, pregnant with itself. I do begin to think that I am in touch with something larger than me, one of the few things. I feel that I am transcribing verbatim from a flow of language running through the room, an ink current into which I dip the pen. It is a dark stream, swift running, a twisting flow that never doubles back. The amazement is that I need only to enter the room at those strange hours to be drawn back into the language. The frustration is that I cannot be there all the time.

Wintergardens

ONE EVENING, OUR THREE- AND FOUR-YEAR-old daughters are playing and I am working half-heartedly at my usual piles of unanswered correspondence. Suddenly, I overhear them.

"God is made out of sky and wind," says the older in a voice of absolute assurance.

"No," the other is equally firm. "A flower. God is a flower."

Outrage ensues. Panic. One threat flies, another. They come to me and I stumble, caught up short and unprepared. I am very much surprised that our

LOUISE ERDRICH

daughters, at such young ages, are wrestling with big questions about the foundations of existence. To solve two mysteries at once, they link God and death. One insists to the other that the reason we must die is so that God can stay alive. If we die, then God must die, the other is certain. They look at me, glaring, questioning. I open my mouth, close it, clear my throat. I have never lied to them. I sort quickly through my beliefs, but I don't have a sound set of reassuring answers. Every organized religion seems to me as much political as spiritual, even my grandfather's caretaking traditional Ojibwa worldview, which is closest to my heart. I can't confirm their hopes about an afterlife, describe God's looks, picture a reliable heaven. Their expressions lower in disapproval. They want certainty, not more metaphysical confusion. At last in a burst of stentorian authority the younger gathers herself and bellows out, *"God's in the garden!"*

Her sister narrows her eyes but then, to my relief, slowly nods. "Church is in the woods," she commands in a low voice, and then, rebellious, "I *have* to believe in heaven." They turn to building a blockhouse together. Maybe, as I'm told at bedtime in a whisper, *God is a white rose that blooms in*

26

winter. I fill my thoughts after they are sleeping with that extraordinary image. From there, next summer's season of flowers catches hold. I become obsessive. Having failed to solve my own religious questions, I feel I must help our daughters solve theirs. As post-Christmas seed catalogues flood the mail, I pile them around my reading chair already awash with religious gropings—everything from *The Interior Castle* to birchbark scrolls, the *Tao Te Ching* to *A Treatise on Angel Magic.* Perhaps proving my daughter right about God's whereabouts, however, I find the seed catalogues most comforting. At last I decide there is no better way to spend these last slow suspenseful evenings than plotting out something spiritually definitive, of the earth, an imaginary garden.

IT IS hereditary. My family has always planted in the wrong season, starting with my licorice-eating Ojibwa grandfather, who provided for a dozen children during the Great Depression from his lush Turtle Mountain Reservation truck farm. Every January, he decided which of his forty rhubarb hills to spade and divide. My Minnesota Polish step-grandmother on my father's side, Mary Korll, burned coal in a building with no running water and kept her geraniums going in coffee cans. These days, with room to spread out, she sorts and cleans seeds saved from the sweetest squash, the tallest hollyhocks. Ziploc bags of her favorites reach me by mail. In December, my mother mentally argues with her flowers too, moving her trellis here, no, there, and sowing her marigolds along the cracked window-wells. And my father, in the arid subzero months when North Dakota is as barren and lifeless as an asteroid, roots hypothetical apple trees of a sturdier variety than those that succumbed to last year's drought, or invents new ways to foil the sweat bees that gut the crunchy little chestnut crabs for sugar.

I have spent my whole life around people who can walk into the backyard and pull dinner from the ground. My parents' back steps in October are stacked with Moregold squash. Bins of tomatoes individually wrapped in torn newspapers, apples sorted into buckets, stuff the garage. Through the winter and into March, my mother can select from her basement shelves an entire preserved harvest sampler, the jars wiped clean, almost luminous in the underground gloom.

I turn to the stack of catalogues crammed beneath my chair. Key pages are folded over, my choices circled with green Magic Marker. Pampas-grass is essential to the new design, a focal center of feathery plumes. The lemon lily circle from a Minnesota friend must be moved to bloom casually against a different boulder. There is the question of which variety of climbing bean will best decorate the six-foot fence that once restrained Michael's high-jumping Siberian husky. Should it be Kentucky Wonder, foot-long pole beans from Jung's, or once again the old-fashioned scarlet runner, which attracted ruby-throated hummingbirds and grew with such startling rapidity its shoots outdistanced the depredations of slugs?

There is that ubiquitous question of pests: which tactics? Last year, my beer bug-traps were lapped up by skunks whose subsequent wild and odorous party kept the south side of the house off limits for a week. The latest slug removal scheme, diatomaceous earth, kills less kindly than spirits. My parents have advised me to wire cups of yeast and molasses to the apple trees, to attract voracious coddling moths. I'll tape egg cases of the aphid-eating praying mantis to the posts of my fence, or release a quart or two of lady-bugs, deliverable by UPS, guaranteed hungry upon arrival. And perhaps swooping purple martins, who devour hordes of mosquitoes, will take up residence next spring in the aviary apartment house we're raising near the pond.

All of this I do, undo, redo, night after night. I am clothed in deep winter. My flesh is packed snow and the only colors in the landscape are the plumages of birds—snappy bee yellow of grosbeaks, arrogant crests of jays, the flames of the cardinals sinking and rising through the scrub alder. Color occupies and feeds the brain. The longing for it is a private and surpassing hunger. In the far north, Ojibwa hunters are sometimes attacked by a hiemal psychosis, the source of which is thought to be the absence of color in the landscape. It is, of course, light that produces color, white light of different wavelengths, frequency, and energy. It has been estimated that human beings can visually distinguish some ten million different colors. No wonder the unrelieved whites and grays of winter, after two or three months, cause restlessness and mental fatigue. Perhaps it is a mild version of this visual need, too, that fuels my obsession to coordinate a summer-long color symphony.

Just as the salmon pink Shirley poppies fade, there will be Missouri primrose, then the heavy spires of delphiniums, against which the magenta phlox will bud, the purple lythrum blaze. Down the borders of the flower bed, among the stones, I'll replenish the orange and gold Iceland poppies, their seeds brought two years ago from the Chateau Lake Louise. I'll keep the collection of wildly painted violas and perennial pansies, grown especially for me by a neighbor with a greenhouse. I plan the most dramatic palette combinations. The sunbursts of coreopsis with azure tufts of ageratum. I have never understood the point of Vita Sackville-West's all-white garden at Sissinghurst. After all this snow, who needs more *whiteness*?

Sipping a cup of steeped chamomile buds, I soothe myself with exotic and enthusiastic catalogue claims. "From Ethiopia come white stars with mahogany eyes." "*Supermale* is so superior to other asparagus it almost defies comparison." Who can resist "a truly great 19th century rose . . . with a rich raspberry aroma"? Australian drumstick flowers, red hot pokers, lilies of Peru. The names themselves are almost intoxicating in their splendor and whimsy. There is a green-throated daylily named thousand voices, and its relatives: tree swallow, parian China, Chicago petticoats, and eenie weenie, a "vigorous, light yellow dwarf." White lightning is a grandiflora rose. Song of Japanese dancing mice, a mauve ruffled iris. Double Persian buttercup, false dragonhead, japonica. Meadow sage, soapwort, and pincushion-flower. Angel's-trumpet, and green envy zinnias. Not to mention the fruits and vegetables, the radishes ranging from French breakfast to Easter egg to round black Spanish, or Sandwich Island mammoth salsify. Yolo wonder peppers. Big moon pumpkins that produce jack-o'-lanterns weighing more than one hundred pounds.

Pearly gates morning glories. Heavenly blues. There is a ring of the biblical in old-time plants like Jacob's ladder, burning-bush, Judas tree, and cosmos. I pick a whole bouquet of the demurely sexual—peacock feather nymph, Essex witch, "a spicily-scented Dianthus with fine fringed petals," climax marigolds, or the "rare and beautiful bleeding heart flower," pantaloons. For the high-minded, there is the Chinese scholar tree, or ivory tower, a white wisteria discovered growing on the campus of Princeton University. I contemplate the tang of unknown fruits. Jostaberry! Can I possibly distill absinthe from the new Burpee's offering, *Artemisia absinthium*, wormwood, a silver-green perennial?

Drowsy with possibilities, I fill the snow-sheeted

yard with crab apple trees, pink and white blossoms studded with bees. I mentally clear new iris circles, sink a pond we've been talking about, build flagstone walks or simply remember the gilded frieze of wild milkweed and goldenrod, the violet asters, August's profusion. These pictures vanquish the frozen monotony and calm me, but of course they also exceed the reality of what will, in truth, turn out to be my garden.

Full of the usual blights, mistakes, ruinous beetles and parasites, glorious for one week, bedraggled the next, my actual garden is always a mixed bag. As usual, it will fall far short of the imagined perfection. It is a chore. Hard work. I'll by turns aggressively weed and ignore it. The ground I tend sustains me in easy summer, but the garden of the spirit is the place I go when the wind howls. This lush and fragrant expectation has a longer growing season than the plot of earth I'll hoe for the rest of the year. Raised in the mind's eye, nurtured by the faithful composting of orange rinds and tea leaves and ideas, it is finally the wintergarden that produces the true flowering, the saving vision.

To dream in the falling snow, to clothe the ground and leaf out trees, to turn the pages of my brilliant trove of flower pictures and gaze into my heart where I can feel and not see, almost touch, a boy or girl whose coloring or features I imagine as watercolors brushed into the edges of a form. My winter summer includes a child lying on a blanket, entranced at the spectacle of light, the arching clouds, the blaze of Arctic flame, a hardy subzero rose I have ordered, and will plant, and which is guaranteed to bloom in this baby's first summer of life.

Famous labors

STILL, IT SEEMS UNFAIR THAT BECAUSE I AM a mammal I am condemned to give birth through the lower part of my body while flowers, though brainless, have the wisdom to shoot straight upward in a pure green rush from unpromising seeds. I don't like needles, the smell of hospital disinfectants, or anything made of stainless steel that looks even faintly surgical. I once fainted as my hair was being cut. Blood tests dismay me and I don't want anyone, even my dear midwife and friend, to approach the most vulnerable part of me with anything sharp. Birth involves basins and syringes and episiotomies. I mention these hatreds of mine in order to assure other women that I am a coward, physically timid, and yet we are all stronger than we think when we are when put to a task.

Yet, why is no woman's labor as famous as the death of Socrates? Over all of the millennia that women have endured and suffered and died during childbirth, we have no one story that comes down to us with attendant reverence, or that exists in pictures—a cultural icon, like that of Socrates holding forth to his companions as he raises the cup of hemlock. In our western and westernized culture, women's labor is devalorized beginning with Genesis. Eve's natural intelligence, curiosity, desire, and perhaps sense of justice cause her to taste the fruit of good and evil, the apple of knowledge. Thereafter, goes the story, all women are condemned to bring forth children in pain. Thus are women culturally stripped of any moral claim to strength or virtue in labor. I have no problem with stoicism, I just think it should be acknowledged. War heroes routinely receive medals for killing and defending. Why don't women routinely receive medals for giving birth?

Or for not giving birth—a decision that, in spite of the focus of this book, is just as profound and inarguably more sensible as our world population burgeons.

My mother bore me in Minnesota on a day of high winds, and although she labored for one whole day and part of another she did not make a sound, so all there was, I imagine, in those spaces between contractions, was the moaning and booming of air. She bore seven children, naturally, refusing drugs at a time they were unsafe for infants, and nursing at a time when the prevailing opinion favored bottle-feeding. She trusted herself to a remarkable degree, and because she did so, she also did the work of deciding for me whether to breast-feed, whether I could get through labor, whether I could trust my own instincts to mother a child.

I relied on her in other ways as well. It was no accident that I looked for a midwife instead of an obstetrician and no wonder that Michael and I met our midwife with a feeling of trust at first sight. Complicated, intelligent, with beautiful dark eyes and a quick, warm laugh, Charlotte Houde, our nurse-midwife, is a professional unafraid to make emotional connections. Over the course of delivering our three daughters, the relationship that we develop becomes both medical and loving. In most Western obstetrical relationships there is little sense of spiritual concern, but Charlotte tends to the entire existence of her patients. With every checkup, through every pregnancy, with every baby, I am able to tell her when I'm thrilled, demoralized, afraid, in a state of anguish I can't articulate. Eventually, she gives me a metaphor that I find helpful during the blackest of moments. She compares the deepest wells of depression to gestation, to a time enclosed, a secluded lightlessness in which, unknown and unforced, we grow.

Passions

CHUCK, THE CHINLESS TOM, WAS A SENSUOUS dark-orange striped cat who married late. He loved a female cat I named Tasmin—a glossy, delicate, completely black and devilishly wild cat who hated human beings. With him, she was transformed. The ardor of Chuck and Tasmin was the result of many years of cats abandoned and gone feral in New Hampshire—these tribes of cats formed cat hierarchies and cat neighborhoods throughout the woods and the old barns, mousing and proliferating until I entered the picture. With our older children, I run an ongoing cat rehabilitation program. With persistence and cunning, using a Havahart wire live-trap, I capture and spay, tame cats, and advertise in the For Free column of the *Claremont Daily Eagle*. My most successful descriptive newspaper ad for a kitten: "cute but strange." We must have taken fifty interested calls.

Chuck and Tasmin are like the Egyptian deities, brother and sister, though from litters widely spaced in years. Their love is a touching constant—they curl together everywhere, on ladders, on hay bales, upon the warmed hood of the car. Their affection for each other deepens through catastrophe. Impetuous Chuck loses his lower lip when he thrusts his head into the bucket of coals just set out from the woodstove. His mouth heals to a rakish leer, a companionable grimace that seems to entrance Tasmin still further. She insinuates herself around him, glares into his eyes. Defending the farm, Chuck comes home beaten up, fur ripped away in blooded tufts, chewed spots on his ears, pleased with himself. He breaks his tail. That heals in a sharp kink. He is extremely affectionate, kneads my lap when petted, his whole body rumbling with cat pleasure.

He does not die of fighting, old age, disease,

hunting, rampant fatherhood, or any of the activities that threaten his life again and again. In late winter, he dies the only way to kill a cat. He dies of wonder.

The foundation of our old farmhouse sits across from a tiny pond—never more than four feet deep, a catchall for run-off water with no exit, a stagnant, exciting, salamander-breeding kidney of coffee-colored water. Periodically, we scrape it down to ledge, hoping that by some miracle the water will clear, maybe a little beach will form, a swimming hole, but it remains itself—secretive, sprouting quick alder and aspen at its edges, freezing to a steel-blue sheet each winter.

Chuck walks out on a patch of thin ice during a sudden drop in temperature—at least, so I gather. It is an uncertain February. Perhaps he is investigating a goldfish rising, one of the ornamental Woolworth's twenty-nine-cent carp released in the pond to grow huge and dreamy slow. Perhaps one of them touches the surface for a gulp of air before settling into stasis on the bottom. Perhaps Chuck jumps after it and then keeps going, descends through the nearly stiff water, his heart stopping as he falls, the water closing molecule by molecule so that he is finally suspended, his paws spread and reaching.

I am quite alone when I find him there. Shoveling the new ice clean to make a skating pond, I see the orange blur, the pumpkin-colored cat in Pumpkin Pond, the name our son gave the farm—the cat and the pond and the goldfish frozen in one scene. Deeper than I can see yet, in the dark, in the quiet, in the green ice, I can still hear my son's voice, calling, for he loved the cat. And as for Tasmin, in the next months she grows heavy and big, her delicate body ripples furiously with kittens. She leaps on my sill to stare at me in questioning fury, then prowls, searching, her body arched and defensive. She hardens her gaze when she sees me, then bolts across the snow, an elegantly flung scarf. Some nights and some days, from beneath the house, she howls in a banshee quaver until I begin to tremble at her weird grief and feel like howling with her.

Stones

ON THE WAY INTO LABOR WITH OUR FIRST natural-born child I was in a fury of cleaning—every spot of dirt made me weep with rage. The cats sliding in and out through the broken foundation of the basement sent me quivering with hatred into the bathroom to stare at myself and ask: *How can a being grow so vast?* Look! There was no part of me unstretched—even my toes were little clubs in my shoes! I was a big, mad, absurd woman stirring food in a pot, writing desperately, trying not to smoke. I whined and roared in the house, alone, after Michael and our older children were gone. I began to scrape at the bathroom sink with a scrubbing pad when calmly, from deep within this great lumbering mound of myself . . . she began to be born.

There was just time to set my hair with electric rollers! I did this, imagining that everybody in the hospital would be inspired to heroic acts of concern for such a well-groomed woman. Our first baby came on so fast that I had to kneel and rock between removing one curler, and then the next. Michael found me on the floor before my beat-up maroon writing chair, hair wild, house clean, in an attitude of furious prayer.

With our next we had time to think, to gather composure in a grove of old white pine. I bent to the ground on impulse to pick up a peculiar reddish stone and had to work to pry it, force it, joggle it loose from the frozen earth like a great tooth. It was a bigger rock than I'd thought. An omen? Yet, her birth was peaceful.

Women's Work

ROCKING, BREATHING, GROANING, MOUTHING circles of distress, laughing, whistling, pounding, wavering, digging, pulling, pushing—labor is the most involuntary work we do. My body gallops to these rhythms. I'm along for the ride, at times in some control and at others dragged along as if foot-caught in a stirrup. I don't have much to do at first but breathe, accept ice chips, make jokes—in fear and pain my family makes jokes, that's how we deal with what we can't change, how we show our courage.

Even though I am a writer and have practiced my craft for years, and have experienced two natural childbirths and an epidural-assisted childbirth, I find women's labor extremely difficult to describe. In the first place, there are all sorts of labor and no "correct" way to do it. I bow to the power and grandeur of those who insist on natural childbirth, but I find the pieties that often attend the process irritating. I am all for pain relief or caesereans when women want and need these procedures. Enduring pain in itself doesn't make one a better person, though if your mind is prepared, pain of this sort—a meaningful and determined pain based on ardor and potential joy—can be deeply instructive, can change your life.

Perhaps there is no adequate description for something that happens with such full-on physical force, but the problem inherent to birth narratives is also historical—women haven't had a voice or education, or have been overwhelmed, unconscious, stifled, just plain worn out or worse, ill to the death. Although every birth is a story, there are only so many outcomes possible. Birth is dictated to the consciousness by the conscious body. There are certain frustrations in approaching such an event, a drama in which the body stars and not the fiction-making mind. In a certain way, I'm jealous. I want to control the tale. I can't—therein lies the conflict that drives this plot in the first place. I have to trust this body—a thing inherently bound to betray me, an unreliable conveyance, a passion-driven cab that tries its best to let me off in bad neighborhoods, an adolescent that rebels against my better self, that eats erratically and sleeps too much, that grows another human with my grudging admiration, a sensation grabber, unpenitent, remorseless, amoral.

Birth is intensely spiritual and physical all at once. The contractions do not stop. There is no giving up this physical prayer. The person who experiences birth with the closest degree of awareness is the mother— but not only am I physically programmed to forget the experience to some degree (our brains "extinct" fear, we are all programmed to forget pain over time, and hormones seem to assist), I am overwhelmed by what is happening to me. I certainly can't take notes, jot down my sensations, or even have them with any perspective after a while. And then, once our baby is actually born, the experience of labor, even at its most intense, is eclipsed by the presence of an infant.

The problem of narrative involves, too, more than just embarrassment about a physical process. We're taught to suppress its importance over time, to devalue and belittle an experience in which we are bound up in the circular drama of human fate, in a state of heightened awareness and receptivity, at a crux where we intuit connections and, for a moment, unlock time's hold like a brace, even step from our bodies. Labor often becomes both paradigm and parable. The story of the body becomes a touchstone, a predictor. A mother or a father, in describing their labor, relates the personality of the child to some piece of the event, makes the story into a frame, an introduction, a prelude to the child's life, molds the labor into the story that is no longer a woman's story or a man's story, but the story of a child.

The first part of labor feels, to me anyway, like dance exercises—slow stretches that become only slightly painful as a muscle is pulled to its limit. After each contraction, the feeling subsides. The contractions move in longer waves, one after another, closer and closer together until a sea of physical sensation washes and then crashes over. In the beginning I breathe in concentration, watching Michael's eyes. I feel myself slip beneath the waves as they roar over, cresting just above my head. I duck every time the contraction peaks. As the hours pass and one wave builds on another there are times the undertow grabs me. I struggle, slammed to the bottom, unable to gather the force of nerve for the next. Thrown down, I rely on animal fierceness, swim back, surface, breathe, and try to stay open, willing. Staying *open and willing* is difficult. Very often in labor one must fight the instinct to resist pain and instead embrace it, move toward it, work with what hurts the most.

The waves come faster. Charlotte asks me to keep breathing *yes, yes.* To say yes instead of shuddering in refusal. Whether I am standing on the earth or not, whether I am moored to the dock, whether I remember who I am, whether I am mentally prepared, whether I am going to float beneath or ride above, the waves pound in. At shorter intervals, crazy now, electric, in storms, they wash. Sometimes I'm gone. I've poured myself into some deeper fissure below the sea only to be dragged forth, hair streaming. During transition, as the baby is ready to be pushed out into life, the waves are no longer made of water, but neons so brilliant I gasp in shock and flourish my arms, letting the colors explode from my fingertips in banners, in ribbons, in iridescent trails—of pain, it is true, unendurable sometimes, and yet we do endure.

Every birth is profoundly original and yet plotted a billion times, too many times. We move into the narrative with medical advice and technological assistance and frail human hopes, and yet we often find ourselves inadequately shaped by culture, by family, by each other for the scope of the work. The task requires mystical tools and helpers. For religions to make sense to women, there should be a birth ritual that flexes and exercises the most powerful aspects of the personality in preparation. Organized Christian religion is more often about denying the body when what we profoundly need are rituals that take into regard the blood, the shock, the heat, the shit, the anguish, the irritation, the glory, the earnestness of the female body.

Some push once, some don't push at all, some push in pleasure, some not and some, like me, for hours. We wreak havoc, make animal faces, ugly bare-toothed faces, go red, go darker, whiter, stranger, turn to bears. We choke spouses, beat nurses, beg them, beg doctors, weep and focus. It is our work, our body's work that is involved in its own goodness. For, even though it wants at times to lie down and quit, the body is an honest hard-working marvel that gives everything to this one task.

In praise of my husband's hair

A WOMAN IS ALONE IN LABOR, FOR IT IS AN unfortunate fact that there is nobody else who can have the baby for you. However, this account would be inadequate if I did not speak of the scent of my husband's hair. Besides the cut flowers he sacrifices his lunches to afford, the purchase of bags of licorice, the plumping of pillows, steaming of fish, searching out of chic maternity dresses, taking over of work, listening to complaints and simply worrying, there was my husband's hair.

His hair has always amazed stylists in beauty salons. At his every first appointment they gather their colleagues around Michael's head. He owns glossy and springy hair, of an animal vitality and resilience that seems to me so like his personality. The Black Irish on Michael's mother's side of the family have changeable hair—his great-grand-mother's went from black to gold in old age, Michael's went from golden-brown of childhood to a deepening chestnut that gleams Modoc black from his father under certain lights. When pushing each baby I throw my arm over Michael and lean my full weight. When the desperate part is over, the effort, I turn my face into the hair above his ear. It is as though I am entering a small and temporary refuge. How much I want to be little and unnecessary, to stay there, to leave my struggling body at the entrance.

Leaves on a tree all winter that now, in your hand, crushed, give off a dry, true odor. The brass underside of a door knocker in your fingers and its faint metallic polish. Fresh potter's clay hardening on the wrist of a child. The slow blackening of Lent, timeless and lighted with hunger. All of these things enter into my mind when drawing into my entire face the scent of my husband's hair. When I am most alone and drowning and think I cannot go on, it is breathing into his hair that draws me to the surface and restores my small courage.

Archery

DURING A TIME OF GRIEF IN MY FATHER AND mother's house, during a period when their adolescent children seemed lighted with a self-destructive fire beyond their control, I found the quote so often used about children written on a scrap of paper in my father's odd and lovely handwriting.

You are the bows from which your children as living arrows are sent forth. . . . Let your bending in the archer's hand be for gladness.

Because my parents for a time practiced archery,

I know what it is to try to bend a bow that was too massive for my strength. In the last stages of labor, gathering into each push and bearing the strange power of transition, a woman bends the great ash bow with an unpossessed power. She struggles until her body finds the proper angle, the force, the calm. The fiberglass, the burnished woods, increase in tension and resilience. Each archer feels the despairing fear it cannot be done. But it will, somehow. Walking in the streets or the trails sometimes, now, looking at the women and their children as they pass, I think of them all as women who have labored, who have bent the bow too great for their strength.

AT LAST, with the birth of each daughter, Michael and I experience a certainty of apprehension, a sensation so profound that I feel foggy brained attempting to describe how, in the first moment after birth, the *actual being* of a new person appears.

We touch our baby's essential mystery. The three of us are soul to soul.

PART II

Spring

Heart

THE FIRST NIGHT OF OUR BABY'S LIFE IS SPENT on her father's chest, held just there, in the bed or the rocking chair. I think of the German expression for the way a pregnant woman carries her child *under her heart*. Now it is Michael's turn to carry our baby over his. And he does. She curls there, hunched in a doll-size flannel gown, a cotton cap. Beside them, my breasts filling painfully, astoundingly, I'm too tender and bumpy to sleep on. So I rest lightly but profoundly, and in exhausted relief. My heart is an ordinary ex-smoker's, so-so-runner's, diligent untroubled ticker, anyway. His is more complex. It beats faster, booms louder, swishes his blood through an extra flourish of artery. Michael's is a diagnosed Wolff-Parkinson-White heart with a more complicated beat. Each daughter finds her first wonder in its samba knock.

The newborn dance

THERE IS A DANCE THAT APPEARS OUT OF nowhere, steps we don't know we know until using them to calm our baby. This dance is something we learned in our sleep, from our own hearts, from our parents, going back and back through all of our ancestors. Men and women do the same dance, and acquire it without a thought. Graceful, eccentric, this wavelike sway is a skilled graciousness of the entire body. Parents possess and lose it after the first fleeting months, but that's all right because already it has been passed on—the knowledge lodged deep within the comforted baby.

Sometimes the dance returns, for moments, when one begs another's newborn child away from other ravished and exhausted parents, but it rarely works. The sway and hop and rhythm are peculiar to your own child, to his or her particular biology and stringed emotion, the harp of nerves.

I KNOW from the first that the babyhood of our youngest will be surprising. Her dance has entered my body—a soul rumba, slow, committed, with a hiccup on the fourth step. She is acutely sensitive, a mine of emotions, an easily saturated sponge for the most minute sensations. She is a cloud of sweeping sadness bunched around a germ of a purely focused will. Her roots into this life are dartlike, fine hairs. She isn't sure that she wants to be here. Unlike her older sisters, who always seemed absolutely positive, she is still making up her mind.

We had planned with this baby to make an even division of infant care, for, as well as parenting and shepherding our older children through school, Michael had been teaching full-time when the other girls were small, and we felt that he'd missed out. We count on combining our experience, but circumstances don't cooperate. Troubled adolescents require the service of a full-time social worker, counselor, tough talker, pleader and finagler—that person is their father. At the same time, we find that we have a smart, touchy, wakeful, breast-fixated baby. And then, too, our life together becomes too big, too unwieldy, too fast. One of us has to manage the shifting complications. The other of us gets our baby.

I confess that, in deep love, I want her, I choose her. I adore the privilege of our babies' constant care even though to write a paragraph requires long preparation. I have never been able to leave our children to their weeping, to let them cry themselves to sleep, as some experts suggest. In order to write, I have to plan ahead. Last night, at eleven, I began with a late feeding in the hope of getting a night of sleep for all of us. Then at three and at six, more feedings, Michael rising to rock and soothe her. At nine A.M. I put her into her bunting and cart her across the road to this little house.

One reason there is not a great deal written about what it is like to be the mother of a new infant is that there is rarely a moment to think of anything else besides that infant's needs. Endless time with a small baby is spent asking, *What do you want? What do you want?* The sounds of her unhappiness range from mild yodeling to extended bawls. *What do you want?* Our baby's cries are not monotonous. They seem quite purposeful, though hard to describe. They are a language that changes every week, one so primal that the meaning I gather is purely physical. I do what she "tells" me to do—feed, burp, change, amuse, distract, hold, help, look at, help to sleep, reassure—without consciously choosing to do it. I take her instructions without translating her meaning into words, but simply bypass straight to action. My brain is a white blur. I lose track of what I've been doing, where I've been, who I am.

Sleeping with stones

EVERY MORNING WHEN I WALK INTO OUR four-year-old's room I greet a complicated sight. She has been up since dawn removing every toy from its accustomed spot: stuffed animals, wooden blocks, barrettes, hair bows, toy beads and broken pieces of games, smashed cars and old Star Wars figures, and other bits of play flotsam washed to the bottom of the toy baskets over the years. All of these things have been removed, arranged, examined, played with. All of these things have been spoken to already, questioned, transformed. She already has a rock collection—that stone I hauled from the ground to touch in labor was somehow a predictor of her desire to touch and carry stones. For a gift, she would rather have a rock than a doll, or a live beetle, which to her is a kind of living, moving pebble. Sometimes she sleeps with a favorite rock (these days pyrite, or a large crystal of amethyst) instead of a stuffed animal.

One morning, I bend to her to wake her from

sleep and find, curled next to the pillow, a tranquil caterpillar. I am sorry to say it is an eastern tent caterpillar, a most destructive pest, but she has taken it to bed to sleep with. It is still living, probably hungry, but not squashed or harmed in the least. I look at her face, so entranced and clinical, so observant, so full of clear compassion for the meek, and I stifle the impulse to murder her pet. We set it free, carry it out the back door and into the grass. Together we watch it crawl away, heading toward my favorite apple tree.

March. Spring storms.
Ravens and wild turkeys.

SHE IS A WINTER-SPRING BABY, AND ALL DAY there is just her, me, snow, and the birds outside. Every morning I dump pans of sunflower seeds, old bread, lumpy oatmeal on a stump in the yard. For the omnivorous ravens, I add a cup of cat food, and for the wild turkeys and the deer, should they ever come near, cracked corn. Of course, most of the deer are far off in their winter yards, or long frozen in a hunter's deep freeze. But three wild turkey hens visit the bird feeder twice a day, at around eleven o'clock and again at three. I am always surprised to see them, sensing before they appear at the edge of the woods their great dark shapes—bundles of rags on stilts. They walk purposefully, elegantly and quickly, toward the apple tree and the corn I've tossed beneath. Sometimes they approach the house. This morning, they pick their way in formation up to the door.

I have put baby down to sleep, still wearing her bright red snow suit, and she has wakened. She is making small dove noises that attract the three hens, who crane their sinuous necks, shake their angry scarred red faces, and raptly stare in at her. We're all caught in fascination, regarding one another. Then the smallest of the hens, who nevertheless is huge, whirls around, takes four long galloping strides, and reaches the edge of the yard. The others watch her with disapproval and annoyance, then lift their three-toed feet delicately and stalk off—rich, dark, irides-cent, leaving shit like rolled cigar ash.

Each morning, too, as we approach the writing studio and riffle of woods, the ravens harshly gossip down at us from a favorite branch in a lightning-cleft white pine, where they have established a nest. Last spring, the oldest two hatched five young and sometime last summer, as we sat idly in the yard tossing sticks for the dog, seven ravens, two full grown and five smaller, ragged teenagers, flew overhead making a commotion. It was easy to see that the parents were giving a flying lesson. There was no mistaking the yells of encouragement, the cries of fear and delight from the fledglings.

Now, almost twelve months later, I sit at the window watching seven huge and handsome black ravens and the three turkey hens, who plunge through the underbrush in loping strides and chase the ravens off their food. The ravens flap in wide bounces, but land only feet away, form a circle, and nonchalantly converge on the irritable hens, plucking bits of cat food and corn from under their splayed feet, adroitly avoiding their outstretched necks and beaks, until the hens have had enough and, as if to salvage some dignity, suddenly ruffle their plumage and pedal back into cover.

The ravens remain as the early spring snow begins to fall through the windless morning air in chains, endless chains. Only three feed at one time. The others sit in the branches, keeping watch or playing fair, according to raven etiquette. Occasionally they descend, their beaks balled with new snow.

The light is brilliant, the snow fluffy and half a foot deep. Hunched and sleek, the largest raven runs the fresh snow up and down the shaft of each feather, then dives once, twice, straight into a drift, body-surfing into a motionless wave. One thing is clear: I am not the only watcher in the woods. Sometimes, as I'm taking notes before the window, in easy view, I feel eyes upon me and slowly look up to see that on the nearest branch a raven sits, intently following the roll of my pen across the page.

The melt

THE SAP IS RUNNING AND THROUGH THE woods and along the roads the maples are tapped, connected by blue plastic lines. On the Great Plains, spring booms in the volume of wind, in the changed angle of sun suddenly warm through the back of your shirt. In the New Hampshire woods, spring is primarily a music, for with the sudden snowmelt filled streams trickle, slide, wash, run, and bounce across the earth and rocks with a satisfyingly pagan exuberance. I am used to the larger movements of nature, and these woods are so full of details. Stands of sugar maple that have been used for hundreds of years now are like a complex body, the blue rubber lines the veins and arteries, the sap a clear blood, a moving tide collected in barrels and hauled off on sledges to fires that seem to beat in and out in the woods like great blasting lungs and hearts.

The Chickadee's tongue

WE SHALL NEVER KNOW HOW OFTEN BIRDS fly into things, whether, in the woods, they misjudge distances rarely or often and crash. My windows are a particular hazard before I paste the cutout shadow of a hawk into the corner of glass. Today a chickadee hits the window with a small, surprising thunk. I walk outside, pluck it off the warming earth. The bird is stunned, blinking, undamaged. I stand motionless with the bird in my hand, examining it carefully, but not a feather seems to have snapped or ruffled. I think of Pretty Shield, a Crow Indian woman interviewed by Frank Linderman before the turn of the century. Her people had great regard for the chickadee, and so do I, for it is a tough, cheerful, weightless survivor of the harshest winters, and its call seems always pleasantly friendly and encouraging. Linderman, professing to know much of chickadees, whistled the little bird's spring song to Pretty Shield. Her face became animated. Then she asked, to his intrigue, if he had seen the chickadee's tongue.

The bird was a calendar to the Crow people. If one forgot the month, one caught a chickadee and looked at its tongue. Through the winter, she said, it develops up to seven tiny bristles in its mouth.

I have always wanted to catch a chickadee and look at its tongue, but now that I've got one, my hands seem as big and clumsy as paws. I don't dare try to open its beak. Regaining its wits, the bird seems to trust me—it vibrates, its breath spins, its heart ticks too fast to apprehend, but it doesn't leave the palm of my hand. I wouldn't close my fingers on it for anything, and it knows. It looks up at me, alert and needle-sharp, but very calm, and I feel suddenly that I am an amazingly fortunate woman.

Crying

WALKING. WALKING. WALKING. ROCKING her while her cries fill me. They rise like water. A part of me has been formed and released and set upon the earth to wail. Her cries are painful to me, physically hard to take. Her cries hurt my temples, my breasts. I often cry along if I cannot comfort her. What else is there to do? This morning she falls asleep, finally, as I rock her. Sucking her favorite three fingers, she drifts. All of the tension leaves her small, round, tender body. She goes heavy against me. In this old chair, woven of tough bent willow, I keep rocking her. My chance to work has come, but I hate to put her down.

I'M AN instinctive mother, not a book-read one, and my feeling is that a baby must be weaned slowly from its other body—mine. So I keep her close, sleep with her curled tight, tie her onto me with padded contraptions. My days here have become sensuous, suffused with the particular, which is not to say that they aren't difficult, or that I get much done. With each birth I have been thrown into a joy of the physical emotions, a religious and fixated delight that seizes me so thoroughly the life of the imagination sometimes seems a spare place. The grounded pleasures—nursing, touching the exquisite fontanel of our baby, a yellow-pink fragrance of sun-heated cotton and tepid cream, gazing eternally into her mystery eyes—are only tempered by sleep deprivation. We know why prisoners break more easily without sleep. *I give up, I'll tell you anything,* I want to say to her sometimes, nearly weeping.

A BABY in a true snit, screaming uncontrollably for hours, can reduce the most loving mother or father to a low extreme. The rise and fall of the voice is primal and relentless. One is driven to exquisite levels of frustration as each remedy fails. There's very little of nonplatitudinous intelligence written on this problem. Even in these millennial times, perhaps, we don't care to admit that we don't live up to the combination Victorian Angel of the House and sixties and seventies Earth Goddess as well as the supremely competent Power Mother of our current age—a woman who is never made helpless by infant dissatisfaction. Men, for all too many reasons, aren't often faced with this problem yet, but will be when at last there is just such a fatherly stereotype to overcome— one that implies too much instead of too little involvement.

Anger or frustration, it comes to the same thing, is a shameful subject when its cause is a physically powerless infant. Yet more honesty would help here. It is no secret that parents cross the line and abuse their children. The extremity of what does happen is part of the habit of denial and the last secret of female and parental anger is anger against the very object of our most protective love. At any rate, when faced with baby's severest crying bouts—and she is a sensitive baby, irritable, intelligent, hair-triggered—I've found it helpful to be an honest hypocrite. Alone with her, beyond tears, shaking sometimes, I use my most soothing tone of voice to call her names. The tone helps her, the words help me.

Watching her tiny, unconscious, tender face, I wonder if my mission to relocate her in this universe, to satisfy her every need, to comfort every trouble, to seduce her into loving life, isn't all just so much rationalizing. I watch her breath deepen, feel her body go limp in bliss, and repeat a lullaby unworthy of a Hallmark card mother.

You're a crank! I whisper, holding her tenderly. *A goddamn crank! You're driving me completely nuts!*

Nests

I HAVE ONE NEST OF EASTERN PHOEBE CON-
struction—mud and emerald moss, a failed attempt
that fell off a too slick wall, a comfortable looking
silver nest constructed of the down of milkweed
pods, a loose swirl of long hairs plucked from the
tails of our neighbor's brown and white horses. I
have the nest of a Baltimore oriole, a long gray sack
with a bottleneck, woven to a budded apple branch, a
very special nest that my father at sixty-eight risked
his neck climbing a high tree to collect for me. I have
a tight little nest including plastic tinsel and my
mother's pink-blue knitting yarn, a heavy robin's
nest of thick muck and flower stems, and a cup of
grass and shredded Kleenex. I suppose I could
include my wasp nests, the silt cones, the paper
bowls, the great gray combed rose I cut from a year-
old sumac. I collect nests in late fall when the leaves
are off the trees. On my shelves, there are quite a few
nests, collected casually year by year. I prize above
them all the nest constructed of my daughters' hair.

My mother gave me the idea two springs ago. I
saw her draping yarn on the flowering crab apple

tree just outside the kitchen window, and the following fall I found the nest containing those very
leftovers from a scarf she had been knitting. All last
winter, just before breakfast each morning, I brushed
the dark brown, the golden, the medium brown hair
of our daughters smooth, and all winter I saved the
cleanings from the brush in a small paper bag that I
emptied by the stump in the yard last spring.

It was not until the leaves fell off and the small
trees bent nakedly beside the road that I saw it, a
small cup in a low shrub, held in the fork of a
twisting branch.

Now, as I am setting the nest on a shelf in the
light of an eastern window, our middle daughter's
blond hair gleams, then the roan highlights in the rich
brown of the eldest's and perhaps a bit of our baby's
fine grass-pale floss. It is a tight woven nest that kept
its shape through the autumn rain. It is a deep cup, an
indigo bunting's water tight nest, perhaps, or a
finch's.

It is almost too painful to hold the nest, too rich,
as life often is with children. I see the bird, quick
breathing, small, thrilling like a heart. I hear its song,
high and clear, beating in its throat. I see that bird
alone in the nest woven from the hair of my daugh-

ters, and I cannot hold the nest because longing seizes me. Not only do I feel how quickly they are growing from the curved shape of my arms when holding them, but I want to sit in the presence of my own mother so badly I feel my heart will crack.

Life seems to flood by, taking our loves quickly in its flow. In the growth of children, in the aging of beloved parents, time's chart is magnified, shown in its particularity, focused, so that with each celebration of maturity there is also a pang of loss. This is our human problem, one common to parents, sons and daughters, too—how to let go while holding tight, how to simultaneously cherish the closeness and intricacy of the bond while at the same time letting out the raveling string, the red yarn that ties our hearts.

My mother is a patient woman. For years, she taught knitting to adolescents. That says it all. She had seven children by age thirty, has fourteen grandchildren now, in her midfifties. When the noise and the heat of young lives overwhelm her, she still cans tomatoes. When she was frustrated, she used to press the pedal of her sewing machine flat, sending the needle into a manic frenzy. She never lashed out at a child. That lesson is profound.

I do not have my mother's patience. In fact, I started out writing poems because I couldn't sit still long enough for longer pieces of fiction. One raw and rainy Baltimore evening, in an apartment that smelled of wet wool and ancient mice, I remembered my great-grandmother Virginia Grandbois. When she had aged past the reach of her own mind, she wanted to walk home. Every day my grandmother, Mary Gourneau, who was caring for her, tied her into her chair to keep her from walking off into the fields and sloughs. I, too, tied myself into my chair to get home the only way I could, through writing. A long scarf, knotted at the waist, allowed me to finish the first pieces of prose I'd ever done. Rewriting took a double knot. Patience never did come naturally, though, and now, to care for our baby requires a skill I do not automatically possess.

To be the mother of an infant, I have to return to the deep ground of the physical, to tie the scarf invisibly around the two of us in dazzling knots. I find it surprisingly difficult, and then, one day, I am invested mysteriously with my mother's grace.

Michael is on a difficult publishing tour and I am alone with our children. This has been a no-sleep week for each of them. At four in the morning of the fourth night I haven't slept, I sit down in front of the phone, weeping. I page through the directory, find Emergency, look for some number to call and even pick up the phone thinking, "911. My baby won't sleep!" At that point, I collapse across my desk, light-headed, laughing, and fall into a fifteen-minute coma before the next round begins.

It happens to be a long crying bout, nothing wrong physically, just growth, maybe teeth. Who knows? Sometimes babies just cry . . . and cry. Morning drags in with a work deadline dead and past for me, our baby continues to cry. Then, in my office, with her in the crib next to the desk, I break through a level of sleep-deprived frustration so intense I think I'll burst, into a dimension of surprising calm.

My hands reach down, trembling with anger, reach toward the needy child, but instead of roughly managing her they close gently as a whisper on her body. As though I am somehow physically enlarged, I draw her to me, breathing deeply. The tension drops away. At this moment, I am invested not with my own thin, worn endurance, but with my mother's patience. This is a gift she has given to me from far away. Her hands have poured it into me. The hours she soothed me and the deep quiet in which I watched her rock, nurse, and comfort my younger brothers and sisters have passed invisibly into me. This gift has lain within me all my life, like a bird in a nest, waiting until the moment my hands need the soft strength of wings.

May nights. Desire.

SPRING DUSK. IT IS THE BLUE OF A SMOKING engine out there, and now, from the pond, the rippling sexual sobs of wood frogs, bullfrogs, the full-throated breathing of the deep night, begin. It is a song so powerful I lay upon the bed pressed into the waves. The air throbs, filled and running over with alluring Spanish *r*'s. This is the night in its entirety— leaves, grass, quaking air. The sound inhabits me, as if the dark passes into me, thrilling and complete. I walk out at midnight to stand within the tension as the moon shows, gleaming and porous, through the stanchions of pine.

Black stalls housing black horses, black grass, black trees, whir of black wings at the back of my head. Waking in the deep blackness, nursing a baby, is the most sensuous of animal tasks. All night I wake, feed our baby, sleep, wake again to the tiny body curled to me in the depth of that seething music.

Duck rape

A COMMOTION OF SPLASHES DRAWS ME OUT to the pond. For weeks, a changing set of mallards has roamed the interconnected swampy places, and now, as I approach the tiny inlet, I see that eight or ten handsome males, green heads iridescent and sleek, are clustered together biting avidly at one another. I think they're fighting over tadpoles, spilled corn, a minnow, and I'm about to turn away when from beneath them a female duck lunges, head balded to pink where the male ducks have torn out her feathers.

I stretch my hands out to grab her—the complete wrong thing to do, for of course I frighten her back toward the water. She throws herself in and is immediately covered in a wild swoon of mallards. Five, six, eight, twelve, the males paddle, wound up, in circles around the male that rides her like a boat.

He sinks her, holding her head under by the nape of the neck to balance himself as he does his sex jig. As soon as he is finished, the others herd her into deeper water. One fights the others off and jumps onto her back. I kick my shoes off, wade in, but there's nothing I can do that won't make things worse. So I retreat, jump from foot to foot on shore.

Two seconds. Five seconds. The longest goes six. They hold her under, take turns, ride her in circles. She surfaces, breasts water once. She is the calm color of brown camouflage, precisely barred and shadowed, the pattern of dry reeds and grasses. The males are striped and painted like wooden toys and there is something toylike about their passion, too. They seem marionettelike, mechanical. Again and again they swarm her, hold her under for so long that I'm sure she'll never rise. Their fierce purpose and avidity hold them silent.

Slowly, incrementally, she inches toward shore. I step back farther, surprised at her toughness. I can't believe she's got the strength left to continue, but she does, even though one male and another and another pound down upon her. Finally, she drives herself up onto the bank, unpausing. She doesn't stop on land to rest but separates herself straightaway from the others, walking in a determined way. She almost strides—fluffing her feathers to appear bigger. Her bald head shines with blood. Behind her, all the male ducks follow at first, but drop away one by one. Suddenly she has a little force field around her, a frail armor of determinations. She ignores them, walking in a straight line, crossing road and yard, bent on following her path.

Morning glories and Eastern Phoebes

EACH SPRING FOR THE PAST EIGHT YEARS, I've nicked the tough morning glory seeds with a knife and pushed them deep into the soil beside the doorway. Now I know exactly how it will happen, how they will grow. For two months, the shoots will twist and creep, flowing at last up the trellis in tiny bursts, then wild, incredible twisting ropes, until finally in the last weeks of summer they'll blare open. With the sun's passage, we will watch the blossoms rotate wide in the morning and shut at dusk like silken valves. Their color will be celestial, bluer than their namesake heaven.

Within and among the flowers, black and yellow

Argiope spiders will set up their webs. They are swift, streamlined, handsome black and yellow with red-orange bands on their legs. Every year they loom four or five webs in the quiet sunstruck windows facing east, right in the middle of the morning glories. The eggs hatched last winter, the young overwintered in their sacs and even now they are dispersing, already in them the knowledge of how male and female will fix and weave their webs together with an unusual seam—a zigzag up the middle, reinforced, as if stitched by a machine.

Walking over to my office, I play a cat and mouse game with a pair of eastern phoebes. The two birds nest every year on a crossbar on the small latticed lean-to outside the door. Each morning, I duck in quickly with baby in my arms, and then all day as I work, they work, building their nest with dabs of mud taken from a low, swampy part of the yard or the pond behind the house. As we all work, as the baby naps restlessly, pouring her cries out from time to time, I learn what they can see, what is in their line of vision. Each time I rise I make myself part of something else—the wall, the door brace—and move with slow care.

The nest sprouts moss immediately and becomes

an emerald cup. The eggs are laid. I can tell because now the female sits as often as she can, her cool gray back smooth above the moss. When she leaves to hunt with the male they perch together on the electrical wire, a graceful duet. They hover and drop on invisible gnats, snatch food from the air, then exhibit the self-satisfied tail bobbing of their species. Discreet birds, I never know it when the eggs do hatch. I can detect no change in his or her behavior.

Two weeks pass and I despair. Though watching carefully, I can see no young. I think perhaps blue jays, the huge feral tomcat that haunts this place, or maybe my own disturbances have doomed the clutch of eggs. And so my curiosity at last overcomes me. One afternoon, when she flies off, I step outside my door and tap my finger lightly on the crosspiece of wood below the nest. At once, four heads shoot out of the nest, beaks open, raving for food.

Luna

IN THE LIGHT OF A SHADED LAMP, GOLD light, in the sighing of the pond through the screen, I am waiting for the night to close over me with its muscle of rain. The sky opens, the black water pours from the leaves just beyond the torn grass of the yard. For an hour there is only the sound of water. And then, when the rain stops, I am visited by a spirit. She drifts toward the lighted screen, powerful and chaste, her great wings whirring like a child's toy, her thick body a pale wedge of velvet.

I turn out the light, and she is gone into the liquid swell of darkness. With a sound like stiff paper rattling, she rises over the roof, whiter, whiter, into the trees. She returns. The next day when I sit down to work before my windows, she clings to the screen just at eye level. Her thick green fairy wings fan the small breeze. Each wing bears an eye lined in black, a washed blue iris, a staring eye like the evil eye charms above the lintels of Greek houses. She is molten green, each wing edged as though in delicate dried blood. She is there all that whole day and there, too, the next morning when I sit down. Her wings are thinner now, rubbed to membranes, the edges torn and eroded. Her great golden fish-spines of antennae tremble.

She will live for a week, mouthless, a being with one clear purpose. All of this ethereal complexity exists to mate and lay eggs, of course. I pity her for a moment and then I don't want to think about her anymore. She's very troublesome! She is a function of her species life cycle. I put down my pen. *Let us interrogate the great apparition, that shines so peacefully around us*, wrote Ralph Waldo Emerson. Sex is the apparition, the engine, the driven inner workings of all that shines and breathes. The need to write and to reproduce are both all absorbing tasks that attempt to partake of the future. Dim wings will close over our conniving brains no matter what and so we lose ourselves most happily in tasks that partake of the eternal. And once we realize that nothing really does, anything can—pulling weeds, picking apples, putting children to bed.

I make a hieroglyph of my desires, assign grand meanings to my wishes, yet I'm miserably aware it's all brain chemicals, moth pheromones, cravings that can be undone with more ease than I would like to allow. Why learn French, I question the moth. The memory of tricky irregular conjugations will one day deconcatenate into meaningless biochemical structures. Consumed by fire, set free to roam the capillary-fed composting network of all life, they will impress no husband, infuriate no Parisian shopkeeper.

The sexuality of spring reminds me too closely

of the old futilities. The crickets and grasshoppers, sawing away with leg fiddles—wooing. The frogs, distinguishing razor-sharp whines from bull bellows—desperate. Each night, the fireflies flash out a Morse code of desire. I will not read it. I know in my heart the message. I know the end result of this dance of brutal fascinations, this love riot. Mallards. Luna moths. I pay a sort of homage to this creature by watching her bathe her short life away in sunlight. I walk outside and stand behind her. I stretch my finger to the tufts of velvet on her back, look into her dark unknowing eyes. At my slightest touch, she arches. Her wings are strong and heavy as a bird's, and the fluted green tail quivers in such sudden strain that I clap my hands away as though burned.

Hide and seek

LIGHT FLOODS OVER THE WORLD, AN UNEXpected light. To the north, clouds march over the massed trees in regular fleets, plump and white. Baby is waking, her sleep a short nap, to complain of her lonely condition. With all of her being, now, she wants other humans. She is pleased as long as she is fed and there is a face to study, preferably a face that she already knows. This month, she has learned three things essential to being a human: she has learned to eat tiny occasional spoons of rice cereal, food other than mother's milk; she has learned to raise herself up straight on arms and toe points, in a push-up that allows her to look over the edge of her bassinet; and she has learned to laugh.

She first laughed at her sister's peekaboo face, popping unexpectedly toward her. It was such a pure sound that we all laughed too. The sound of her laugh gives everybody pleasure, and so we all encourage her to make the sound again. We experiment. What causes her laugh is this: a combination of the new and the expected with a hint of fear thrown in. Just at the moment she is afraid that your face won't appear, her expectation collapses. When you do appear she laughs the loudest.

The source of laughter lies in anxiety from the very first. Aside from the chuckle of bears, we are famously the only animal that finds this world a source of humor. By what marvel? Laughter is our consolation prize for consciousness. The capacity for humor develops alongside the knowledge that familiar faces vanish. Long before we speak its name, then, we know loss, and recall in ourselves the charm of hilarity that draws our loved ones back to light.

Woodchuck punctuality

EVERY DAY AT EXACTLY 11:45, A FAT GRAY-brown woodchuck ripples across the yard from under the house. I have heard, and now I know it is true, that one can tell time by the habits of wood-chucks. As though she punches a time clock or sets her alarm, this mother woodchuck goes out for lunch at the same moment of the day, every day. There is a patch of clover on the far side of the grass, white stems budding. And of course there are plump gold dandelions that I do not bother to eradicate. The woodchuck, whose name comes from the Cree *wuchak*, not from chucking wood, is a naturally swift and polite eater. Plucking one flower at a time, she holds it by the stem and bites the head off, chews it up, fiercely, quickly, then munches the stem in short bites right down to her small, black, leathery fists.

She picks another and another until she's full. Lunch over, she flows back, an undulating foot rug. Her work is digging holes. The ground beneath the woodshed tacked onto this house is almost on the verge of caving in. Her burrow is probably thirty to forty feet in length, and surely she has more than one nesting room from years past, lined in tufts of winter grass and her own fur, pulled and pressed into the walls.

For my thirtieth birthday, I was given a watch by a dear one who assumed with cheerful lovingness that, since I had never worn a watch, I would now like to start. I smiled and appreciated, but deep down I felt uneasy. Wear a watch? Early on in my adult life I tried to wear a watch, but I didn't like the feel of time ticking itself away on my wrist, as if in a mortal race with my own pulse. I tried to tell time by the length of light, but I was always late. I resorted to keeping the watch in my pocket, where it was easy to forget. Even now, I only wear a watch to travel and to keep appointments with friends.

Still, I'm usually a bit late and relieved if others are a little late too. For some reason, waiting, even alone and conspicuously, doesn't bother me as much as it seems to bother others. Life comes on you all unawares while you are stuck in an interim situation. Life sneaks up. You have a tea, another tea, watch the water, the goldfish in the Chinese restaurant, cadge a cigarette, the first you've smoked in six months. There is the sweet self-indulgence of reading in public, a newspaper! Sometimes I simply feel myself vitally alive in the moment, the interstice. My brain shakes itself like an apple tree surprised by rain, and there, on my empty plate, an idea. I carry pens, paper. I've had friends come up to me, apologetic, and I am annoyed now not that they're late but that they showed up at all to disturb the delicate disequilibrium I've found in waiting.

Fortunately, not long after I received the timepiece I developed an allergy to metal and broke out in red bumps where the watch touched my wrist. Perhaps it is true I am allergic to time itself. At any rate, I find these days that I can tell time well enough by woodchuck. My working day's half over once the fat lady eats her flowers.

Fiddlehead garden

THERE ARE DAYS AND WEEKS WHEN THE only person I see other than family is our mail carrier, John McCauley, a lithe, handsome elderly postal worker who drives a red Subaru with passionate expertise. Over the years, small details pile up between us—snatches of conversation, awaited packages, our stories. We become friends, sustaining each other with small gifts. In his backyard, John has cultivated a garden of wild edible ferns. He and his wife, whom he still mourns with energy and devotion, dug the ferns, brought them home in buckets, planted them, nourished and divided them into a wide bed terraced with field rocks. Before it uncurls in spring, the fern resembles the endpiece of a violin. John's wife loved to eat fiddleheads. He lost her in a senseless accident. Together they had also planted a front yard crocus patch in letters that spelled Welcome Spring. After she died, John stamped out the early blooms, ground them into the frozen dirt. But he kept the fiddleheads, and now he cuts them for neighbors and for me. Every spring, he harvests Ziploc bags of them and leaves them in our mailbox.

The young, brilliant green, still-coiled heads of ferns are a spring tonic that also taste to me of grief. There is no use saying otherwise—they are bitter, no matter how fixed. Boiled, sautéed, steamed, buttered, lemoned, garlicked, onioned, or otherwise, they retain a stringent and delicate flavor that is, to me, quintessentially of New England. I crave fiddleheads in spring, very fresh ones, and I eat them by the bowl. When I've finished great quantities, I find that baby loves me more, craving the slight oddness of fiddlehead milk, spring milk, and also perhaps the edge of sorrow.

STEAMED FIDDLEHEADS FOR MOTHER'S MILK

It is all in the freshness of the fiddleheads. They should be tightly coiled and very green. Remove any of the brown papery husks still on them and wash them. Put them into a steamer pot and boil the steamer water. When the fiddleheads have turned a brilliant green, before they begin to dull, lift them out. They should be slightly firm but not crisp, and soft in the middle of the coil. Dry the fiddleheads. Melt butter, sauté a fresh white onion with two or three cloves of garlic, add the fiddleheads, warm, and toss with lemon juice.

Finches and the Grand Sky

EVERY SO OFTEN, AS I'M WORKING, I THINK I see from the corner of my eye a dandelion burst into the air from the tall grass before me. I finally put down my pen and sit still for a moment and see, then, that it is a male goldfinch. His wife is olive-green, I see her too now, but my eyes follow the male for he is of the exact brightness of the dandelions. He is jumping up and down among them, bouncing on the stems, like a tiny child on the playground. But as I watch closely I see that his business is more serious. He is plucking from the centers of the flowers the softest bristles to use in the nest that the two are building somewhere in the sun-brushed entrance to the woods.

I do not investigate the nest building further, but all day I imagine the color of the nest. Until the dandelion floss dries to paler gold, the nest will be a tiny radiance, a cup of sunlight. I picture the female goldfinch settling herself into a nest the color of her husband and suddenly I think—*that's what I've done, moving to this, my husband's farm.* All around me, kind trees and slabs of rocky land, violet and archaic gold shadows that Maxfield Parrish painted into his *Saturday Evening Post* covers. This is a beautiful place but it is not where I belong. Over and over, in anguish, in hope, we utter the same lines in a long established argument.

"I'm homesick," I keep saying
"This is home," he keeps answering.
Each of us is absolutely right.

Horizon Sickness

AT FIRST, THE ENTIRE NORTHEAST SEEMS
like the inside of a house to me. The sky is a small
ceiling and oddly lit, as if by an electric bulb. Even
here, against the side of a hill, the sun does not pop
over the great trees for hours—and then sinks down
so abruptly. I am suspicious of Eastern land: the
undramatic loveliness, the small scale, the lack of sky
to watch, the way the weather sneaks up without
enough warning.

The woods themselves seem bogus—every inch
of the ground turned over more than once, and even
in the second growth of old pines so much human
evidence. Rock walls run everywhere, grown through
and tumbled, as if the dead still have claims they
impose. The unkillable and fiercely contorted trees of
old orchards, those revenants, spook me when I walk
in the woods. The blasted limbs spread a white lace
cold as fire in the spring, and the odor of the blos-

soms is furiously spectral, sweet. When I stand beneath the canopies that hum and shake with bees, I hear voices, other voices. What they are saying? Where they have come from? What drove them into this earth?

Then, as often happens to sparring adversaries in 1940s movies, I fall in love.

Wild

SIMULTANEOUSLY WITH THE BIRTH OF EACH baby, as if the obstacle of close confinement makes me aware of greater freedoms in the woods, the impulse to get outside hits me, strengthens, becomes again a habit of thought, a reason for storytelling, an uneasy impatience with walls and roads. At first, when I have that urge, I want to get into a car and drive fifteen hundred miles to get back into a place that I define as out. The West, or the edge of it anyway, the great level patchwork of chemically treated fields and tortured grazing land, is the outside I've internalized. In the rich Red River Valley, where the valuable cropland is practically measured in inches, environmental areas are defined and proudly pointed out as stretches of roadway where the ditches are not mowed. Deer and pheasants survive in shelter belts—rows of Russian olive, plum, sometimes evergreen—planted at the edges of fields. The former tall grass prairie has now become a collection of mechanized gardens tended by an array of air-conditioned farm implements and bearing an increasing amount of pesticide and herbicide in each black teaspoon of dirt. Nevertheless, no amount of reality changes the fact that I still *think* of eastern North Dakota as wild.

In time, though, *out* becomes outside my door in New England. By walking across the road and sitting in my little writing house, surrounded by trees, thick plumes of grass, jets of ferns, and banks of touch-me-not, or just by looking out a screen door or window, I see what there is to see. The smothering woods that has always seemed part of Northeastern civilization—more an inside than an outside, more like a friendly garden—reveals itself as forceful and complex. The growth of plants, the lush celebratory springs, make a grasslands person drunk. The world turns a dizzy green, the hills ride alongside the roads like comfortable and flowing animals. And yet, even though I finally grow closer to these woods, on some days I still want to tear them from before my eyes.

I want to see. Where I grew up, our house looked to the west. I could see horizon when I played. I could see it when I walked to school. It was always there, a line beyond everything, a simple line of changing shades and colors that ringed the town, a vast place. That was it. Down at the end of every grid of streets: vastness. Out the windows of the high school: vastness. From the drive-in theater where I went parking in a purple Duster: vast distance. That is why, on lovely New England days when everything should be all right—a spring day, for instance, when the earth has risen through the air in patches and the sky lowers, dim and warm—I fall sick with longing for the horizon.

I want the clean line, the simple line, the clouds marching over it in feathered masses. I suffer from horizon sickness. But it sounds crazy for a grown woman to throw herself at the sky, and the thing is, I want to enjoy what is really here. And so to compensate for horizon sickness, for the great longing that seems both romantically German and pragmatically Ojibwa in origin, I find solace in trees.

Trees are a changing landscape of sound—and the sound I grow attached to, possible only near large deciduous forests, is the great hushed roar of thousands and millions of leaves brushing and touching one another. Windy days are like sitting just out of sight of an ocean, the great magnetic ocean of wind. All around me, I watch the trees tossing, their heads bending. At times the movement seems passionate, as though they are flung together in an eager embrace, caressing each other, branch to branch. If there is a vegetative soul, an animating power that all things share, there must be great rejoicing out there on windy days, ecstasy, for trees move so slowly on calm days. At least it seems that way to us. On days of high wind they move so freely it must give them a cellular pleasure close to terror.

I WANT to fly, to breathe the great rolling sky of the plains. I want to scatter the lovely colors of the nest. But loving this family as I do, I do the opposite.

Instead, I sink roots. With ferocity and purpose and a tenacity that resembles joy, I do in fact settle into the planting of my imaginary garden. In the tradition of my grandmother, using her seeds, I literally transplant myself into this ground and find at the same time that our five-year-old has inherited the gardening urge—she's a ferocious planter, digger, weeder, fellow obsessive planner. To get everything she wants in her garden, she veers between dreamy excitement and practicality. In the local hardware store she pulls me to the seed rack. She insists on: Hollyhocks. Dianthus. Morning glories. Sweet william. Bay. Asparagus. Blue columbine and bleeding hearts.

She loves the most dramatic and complicated growth. I show her how to gently loosen the curled tendrils of root-bound bedding plants. Her capable hands cup the roots, mimic mine. She believes we die but all things are connected, that time goes back and forth, that she could live backwards and be born again, that most things are vaguely aware. She decided to be a veterinarian, thinking it means *vegetarian*, but anyway won't eat anything that ever had a dream. She is tough, already pushing roots into drinking position, tamping down earth around a favorite velvet purple pansy.

"Plants are very trusting," she observes.

Baby strapped across my chest, I brush my face absently with a paw. *God's in the garden.* Our four-year-old gazes long into the kingdom of beetles and keeps her pet cricket fed with peanut butter. Later, after everyone is in bed I find I'm weeping. I've helped our daughters sink roots here too. Perhaps if we water these peonies, these clumps of red sedum, these pensees, these tiny bleeding hearts, maybe if I water my asparagus bed with tears, I'll grow real roots, I think, caught up in the abject melodrama of the exile. Maybe if I dig and fertilize I'll flourish, I'll belong where I am.

Shut up and watch us grow, say the trees.

Soon flowers aren't enough, or vegetables, or shrubs. I have a friend named Ruth who runs a greenhouse in an offhand way—since her husband's death she's been on a mission to propagate the legendary white forsythia that he developed, and she hasn't much time for customers. She sells us trees that have grown from their root balls and perennials I must unroot from beds where they've already taken hold. Japanese tamaracks, white pines, a mulberry tree for the birds. Silver poplars and a catalpa with a surprising great sweet potato of a root and only one tiny shoot on top.

Our oldest son digs the holes—he's very good at digging holes, and there is an art to it that he attends to seriously. He will dig a hole with a beautiful rounded shape, levering rocks out, chipping away the dirt with an infinite patience. He will dig a hole until he's standing in the bottom. His hands are long and fine, cracked on the knuckles, dry and strong. He loves the one-mindedness of it all, the task's finality and seriousness. Together, once the holes are dug, we wrestle trees from the car's trunk, bargain trees, expansive and hearty yew, matching Scotch pines and old fragrant tough New England rosebushes. He digs a fifty-dollar hole for a five-dollar tree, just like it says in all of the planting guides.

Once, after the hole is dug, the two of us shove and push and gradually maneuver a giant yew shrub to the edge. We push it over because it is too heavy to lift and it falls in with a grand thump. Disappears. Only the tips of its branches show a few tiny red berries. The hole was dug deeper than the enormous plant, and we couldn't tell because we were so eager that we planted way past dusk. We fall over, laughing crazily, exhausted. We plant the biggest trees that we can lift, on the theory that we're years ahead, but I'm wrong. Visiting my grandmother Mary Korll of the seeds in bags and the leggy geraniums, I ask what she'd like for a birthday present.

She's a little weaker than I've ever seen her, and she's tending fewer chickens and no geese at all. Still, though she hasn't got a lifetime left to see a tree into maturity, she asks for a two-year cottonwood.

"I want a small one," she says, eyeing me with the old ferocity. "Be sure you get a little one. They take hold the best."

Foxglove. Women of the house.

ABSURDLY, I BEGIN TO CHAFE AT THE AGE OF New England houses. Where I come from out west, almost none are older than the people. Here they outlive us and have contained many deaths. Within these walls, nothing happens for the first time. Knowing that I will one day join the ranks of Yankee ghosts, I am uneasy, unmoored. I'd rather die in the familiar landscape where the grave markers of my recent ancestors stand crooked in the deep mold of oak leaves, or where they are part of the landscape itself, as Ojibwa once buried their dead high in the bones of trees.

I acquire an old portrait of this house and its inhabitants, taken by an itinerant photographer in 1891. I do not know exactly where the people in the picture of this house were buried, but I live where they lived and sleep in the oldest room, so I cannot help but think of them—the woman, in particular.

She stands rigid, hands clasped on her waist, hair pulled into a severe bun. Although she frowns neutrally at the camera, she is surrounded by flowers. Her eyes are sullen in a shadow cast by full-on sun. What have we in common?

My children, like hers, have polished the beautifully fit and rubbed pine floor of this house with the knees of their pants. My children, like hers, gouged the pine knots larger with their forks, dropped pennies into the cracks between the boards, and slept in their parents' arms while all together we paced the predictable creaks. I know this house—the smell of old pine boards in the heat of summer, crumbling basement of mold and shale, the bitter odor of chimneys when the creosote flakes, the tension and friction of wind in the eaves and windows. I know this house—so did the woman in the picture.

This house is sided with wooden clapboards we have knocked free of wasps and barn spiders. The foundation is layered shale and granite hugged from the surrounding earth. My first writing office was once her summer kitchen, and even then its plaster walls must have exuded a damp sweat. As far as we can tell, the first quarter of the house was built in the late eighteenth century. A fire in the local courthouse has destroyed the earliest records of its owners, but sometimes I imagine, beside the door, a small plaque inscribed with the date 1782.

Those numbers have stuck in my head for so long that I have come to measure history around them: near the time that the foundation stones were prized from this farm's fields, Russia annexed Crimea. Beaumarchais presented *The Marriage of Figaro*, and the Articles of Confederation were ratified. All land west of the Appalachians was still Indian territory and the people from whom I am descended on my mother's side, the Ojibwa or Anishinabe, lived lightly upon it, leaving few traces of their complicated passage other than their own teeth and bones. They levered no stones from the earth. Their houses, made of sapling frames and birchbark rolls, were not meant to last.

1782. Coins were placed beneath each corner beam of this house so that its inhabitants would always have money. The walls were raised, the beams hand-cut, the floors laid of virgin pine. A thirty-foot well was dug out back of the kitchen door, a well that went dry only after the invention of enchilada TV dinners.

A hundred years pass. 1882. The daughter of the

man who built the house had grandchildren. The British took Egypt. Close to two million people lived in Paris, and Germany had unified under Bismarck. On my father's side, the Erdrich family migrated west from Austria, settled in the Reichstal, converted from Judaism to Catholicism. 1882. They raised a Bauernhof that still stands in the Black Forest. The last of the Indian treaties were signed, opening up the West. Most of the Anishinabe were concentrated on small holdings of land in the territory west of the Great Lakes. The Turtle Mountain people wore trousers and calico dresses, drove wagons, spoke their own language, but also attended Holy Mass.

1992. Spring. Groundwater seeps through the moss brown basement walls. I pull a wild kitten from the loose rocks of the foundation.

Wild kitten

IT WAS AS IF THE HOUSE ITSELF HAD GIVEN birth. One day the floor cried where I stepped on it, and I jumped back. I was near the heating vent, and when I bent and pried the cover off and thrust my hand in, I grabbed a ball of fur that hissed and spat. I heard the kitten scrambling away, the tin resounding like small thunder along the length of its flight.

I went down looking for it with a flashlight, but of course, at my step the untamed creature fled from the concrete-floored area and off into the earthen crawl space draped with spiderwebs as thick as cotton, a place of unpeeled log beams, the underside of the house. I put out milk in a saucer. I crouched on the other side of the furnace, and I waited until I fell half asleep. But the kitten was too young to drink from a dish and never came. Instead she set up, from just beyond where I could catch her, a piteous crying that I could hardly stand to hear.

I went after her. The earth was moldy, a dense clay. No sun had fallen here for over two centuries. I climbed over the brick retaining wall and crawled toward the sound of the kitten. The big, peculiar, plump gray spiders that live along the eaves and foundations of houses on this road made my throat clench, but brushing through cobwebs I forced a part of my mind shut and concentrated on the cry of the little animal. As I neared, as it sensed my presence was too large to be its mother, it went silent and scrabbled away from the reach of my hand. I brushed fur though, and that slight warmth filled me with what must have been a mad calm because, when the creature squeezed into a bearing wall of piled stones I inched forward on my stomach. I followed with my flashlight the streak of fur, the glowing marble eyes. My back was now scraping along the beams that bore the weight of the whole house above me. Tons and tons of plaster, boards, appliances, and furniture. This was no crawl space anymore. I could hardly raise my shoulders to creep forward, could only move by shifting my hips up and down. On the edge of sickening panic, I had never been in a space so tight, one thought pressed in: If I heard the house creak, if it settled very suddenly upon my back, my last crushed thought would probably be, "Shit! I don't even *like* cats." Because I don't like cats, I just find their silken ways irresistible. Case in point. There I was. I couldn't leave this one to wail in the dark beneath the house.

Its face popped out and vanished right in front of me. How far back did the piled rock go? If I moved a rock would the whole house fall on me? I couldn't think. I reached for the kitten, missed, reached again, missed. I tried to breathe, to be patient. I waited, put myself into suspended animation. Then, after a time, the kitten backed toward me, away from a clump of dirt I threw at the far wall. Its tail flicked through a space in the rocks and I snatched it. Held it, drew it toward me. Out it came with a squeak of terror, a series of panting comic hisses, a whirl of claws and teeth, tiny needles it didn't yet know how to use.

SHE is a delicate creature, fierce and avid a hunter as ever was, a mouser, colored in calico marbled evenly with orange and black. Rocky is her name, and she is the last kitten of the lovers Chuck and Tasmin. At this moment she sits near, glares as I write, leaps into the warmth of my chair when I leave, and is jealous of the baby.

THE night after I pulled her from under the house, the darkness pressed down on me until I woke. I'd swum weightlessly into a smaller and smaller space. What the body remembers of birth it anticipates as death. In the house of my dreams the basement is the most fearful: the awful place filled with water, the place of both comfort and death. I fear in particular the small space, the earth closing in on me, the house like a mother settling its cracked bones and plumbing.

Earlier that afternoon, from underneath, I had heard the house all around me like an old familiar body. I hadn't told anybody else that I was going after the kitten, so nobody knew I was below. The normal sounds of my family's daily life were magnified. Their steps trailed and traveled around me, boomed in my ears. Their voices jolted me, their words loud but meaningless, warped by their travel through the walls and beams. Water flowed through invisible pipes around me, hitched and gurgled. It was like being dead, or unborn. I hadn't thought about it then, but now I could clearly see part of me, the husk of myself, still buried against the east wall: a person sacrificed to ensure the good luck of a temple, a kind of house god, a woman lying down there, still, an empty double.

Fairy tales. Love, grief, and invisible seeds.

HOW MANY WOMEN ARE BURIED BENEATH their houses? How many startling minds, how many writers? This house is over two hundred years old. How many women lie stunned within its walls? It is a new phenomenon that so many women bear and raise children and do work in the outside world. Again, the photograph. I examine the woman's face, her stance between the spires of hollyhocks. I imagine her, and I wonder. A woman needs to tell her own story, to tell the bloody version of the fairy tale. A woman has to be her own hero. The princess cuts off her hair, blinds her eyes, scores her arms, and rushes wildly toward the mouth of the dragon. The princess slays the dragon, sets off on her own quest. She crushes her crown beneath her foot, eats dirt, eats roses, deals with the humility and grandeur of her own human life.

I never could contain myself, never could step back. And yet, the writing that ate me up, that saved my life, drove me over the brink, caught me flying off the cliff by the neck of my shirt, will not be my story in this house. Writing that choked me, writing that gave me everything and took away my peace of mind. Writing, too, that I did with my husband. No, that will not be the story told here.

Blind will without direction. Stubborn and insufficient love. Bewildering love. Helpless and devouring love of children. Forged love, married love, love that starts molten and throughout its life must be thrown back into the fire, recast, reshaped, restored. Some-

THE BLUE JAY'S DANCE

times a vase, a startling beast, a perfect shoe, there is no predicting the raw shape of love when it drops from the burning mold. Married passion is a quest, in the end, and the lovers are its heroes, fighting along the way demons of their own making and of others, changing identities, carving their initials into each other's hearts.

Love is necessity, all else about it is up for grabs. Love's hold is primal, its manifestations baroque, arcane. In the tended garden of the personality or soul, love is the weed of startling loveliness. Flowers of a more acceptable configuration—duty, kindness, citizenship, concern—may take deliberate root and bloom. But love needs no planting, it is sown by wind.

We cannot choose who our children are, or what they will be—by nature they inspire a helpless love, wholly delicious, also capable of delivering startling pain. That weed, again. Some children are best cherished when lightly held, some need to test the strength of your grip. We all grow thorns. We have to. Otherwise our hearts would simply adorn a series of common rooms, plucked and stuck in jars. No, we are too fearfully alive, too stubborn, to yield to just any hand.

"Love is filled with itself," said St. Bernard. "It

overcomes and transforms all other dispositions."
Love is not political. Love resists correctness and
blindly goes on, selecting for smell and touch. We can
bite down hard, hang on to our emotions, get
therapy, but still, love is filled with itself. We can
choose whom we live with, whose hand we shake,
whose cheek we kiss, but we cannot choose who in
this wide world, out of the millions, we truly love.
Our emotions ride air currents whose sources we
cannot name.

Love is an infinite feeling in a finite container,
and so upsets the intellect, frustrates the will. An
anarchic emotion that transcends rules of age, race,
blood, passionate love has a wild philosophy at base.
Because we can't control the fixation of love and
desire, we experience emotional mayhem—stories,
fiction, works of art result. Love's combination of
attraction and despair thrills us. Our peculiar ability
to be at home in the arms of one person, while
always a stranger in the presence of another, is an
ongoing human mystery. Without love, we might
come close one day to knowing how to tinker with
and even set the vast microscopic machinery of our
emotional complex. Love makes such an enterprise
hopeless, a fool's own task.

But even love is not the story here, not what will survive us, or me.

The tale that will live on is the same that survives the other woman, that is, the narrative of flowers. Over the years, I have seen her hand in the places where plants still bloom. In the picture, she stood next to hollyhocks, but those are gone. Beside the door, she planted white phlox of an old variety immune to mildew. The phlox is unkillable, as are her French lilacs, just across the tumbled stone pile. Leggy, pipped, unpruned, they still give off rich perfume. Next to them, beneath an old bent-elbowed apple tree, the ground is a wealth of tiger lilies—hers, I know. And there, at the margin of the lawn, in the waste of grass, a clump of butter yellow jonquils. Hers too the forsythia that must be fiercely restrained by cutting, an old rugosa rose, and perhaps even the two old willows beneath which our family was joined.

In my mind, at least, the woman of this house is responsible for these remnants, these surviving blossoms. In her honor I have nurtured and divided the white phlox so that it now spreads into the backyard, into my circular garden, flares up the sides of the rock walls. It is enthusiastic, bold, tough, and nothing gets it down. But more than any other flower, it is the stately foxglove—blooming biennially, raising a tall cone of purple throats, deeply speckled and thinly furred—that reminds me of the other woman. It is that flower that I think of one winter when I finally receive, from her own hands, as if our two ghosts spoke, a message. Written on a scrap of paper nibbled by mice, embossed with a tiny picture of the capitol building in Concord, found slipped against a thick pine stud when one of the walls is torn up to be rewired, the note reads:

Many persons think the lapse of Time not only softens mourning grief, because of the death of loved Ones, but lessens it to such a degree as in many cases makes the mourner *forget the Grief*—but in your case and mine Dear Mrs. B, I am of the opinion that Time, passing away, but the impression of our grief the stronger makes, as streams their channels deeper wear.

The rest is yellowed holes, as if it had lain under snow, as if its own acids had devoured it. So with our sorrows, so with the mystery of this woman's personal loss. Grief blinds us to itself, plunges under, moves through our arms into the earth, and surfaces in moments out of time. Grief is alchemy by which living memory changes the daily lead and silver of our loved one's existence to purest gold. We caress air, murder hope, wishing for just one ordinary word. Loss is a powerful wave that hurls us forward at the same time that its undertow drags us down, scrapes us along the bottom.

And she is right, the woman of this house. Time passing away but the impression of our grief the stronger makes, as streams their channels deeper wear.

I DON'T really know if Mrs. B planted that mournful biennial, missed it in the off years, knew it would come back the following summer. I only know that foxglove, a flower that would look well in a spray laid across a gravestone or pinned to a black church bonnet, best expresses the slate-hearted gaze that meets mine in the old portrait. And so it is the foxglove I am most careful not to disturb. And it is the foxglove—the sandlike seeds sown in flats each spring, its deadly poisonous leaves the source of the cardiac medication digitalis, that I keep for her and multiply with slow perseverance, as if in the presence of the foxglove these ghosts are not so much laid to rest as still able to partake of the rich and rooted fullness of this life.

PART III

Summer

Job descriptions

SOME DAYS IT SEEMS THAT I HAVE NOT PUT her down for weeks. I am her existence, after all, the way she gets what she wants, the outlet, the method, the tool of her need. Sometimes I hold my child in one arm, nursing her, and write with the other hand. With no separation of thought and physical being, there are times I live within a perfect circle.

Then there are the other times. Months go by and with the end of spring the dim realization surfaces—I cannot concentrate on one thought, one idea. Our baby's slumbers have shortened until she's become a catnapper, sleeping for irregular, short periods. Her rhythms are necessarily mine, too, and so I've found that allowing the mind to fuse with itself, to solve a task, is not so much a luxury as a mental necessity, like dreaming. The primary parent of a new infant loses the ability to focus, and that in turn saws on the emotions, wears away the fragile strings of nerves.

Hormones, milk, heaviness, no sleep, internal joy, all jam the first few months after a baby is born, so that I experience a state of tragic confusion. Most days, I can't get enough distance on myself to define what I am feeling. I walk through a tunnel from one house to the other. It is dark, scraped out of the emotional mess of life, as gray and ridged as an esophagus. I'm being swallowed alive. On those days, suicide is an idea too persistent for comfort. *There isn't a self to kill,* I think, filled with dramatic pity for who I used to be. That person is gone. Yet, once I've established that I have no personal self, killing whatever remains seems hardly worth the effort. For those dark and stupid days, I have developed a mantra to ward off the radical lack of perspective which is also called depression. The chant, absurdly, goes something like this:

I don't have to wear panty hose to work.

I don't have to wear high heels.

I think back to my other jobs in order to get perspective. I know that I am lucky I can have my baby with me and do, at least, some of the work I love. I couldn't have her with me if I still rose at five to catch the truck at six and hoe sugar beets, shedding clothes as the sun arches to its severe height. She'd probably like selling popcorn with me at the movie theater but she'd balk at cleaning the butter machine with pink soap after the last feature. We couldn't life-guard, pick cucumbers, or sell Kentucky Fried Chicken. I would have to leave her with someone else if I still reshelved library books, flipped eggs and pancakes as a short-order cook, served Sacher torte at the pastry shop in Brattle Square, or if I still hauled gravel and weighed dump trucks or tied steel. I couldn't take her with me on the job I had one long year that required fitting on rubber-soled white shoes, a white polyester uniform, then walking over to the locked ward of the state mental hospital to start the day by stripping the night-soiled beds of insane women.

I keep thinking about that last job, psychiatric aide, because part of my task was to talk with delu-sional patients and reflect back my own supposedly normal perceptions of reality. I was twenty years old, walking corridors and steam tunnels with anxious and hallucinating people, explaining, *No, nobody blew spiders underneath your door through a straw last night. I've tucked away my little busts so you can't see them. No, this isn't Harrow, England. You cannot enter the mulatto kingdom. That is not human flesh, it is only turnips. You are not an angel, you are not General Eisenhower in civilian clothes and no, last night you were not artificially insemi-nated.*

I understood from the job that we carry around a private hell that can be activated by a change in brain chemistry. I now, in an odd turnaround, think of the patients often because they do for me what I once did for them. They reflect back perceptions of reality. I measure myself against true schizophrenia and clin-ical depression and find that although my thoughts fray and I'm afraid of my emotions I still am, more than anything, a frustrated writer sleeplessly in love with her third baby.

Whom I don't want to leave, even though this job is difficult.

Every day parents tear their hearts out because they have to leave an infant, a new child with whom they will have a relationship that will very likely last longer than the one they have with each other.

Any sublime effort has its dark moments. Per-haps, if anything, the meaning in this book for others may be this: Here is a job in which it is not unusual to be, at the same instant, wildly joyous and pro-foundly stressed.

Gravity Well

I AM DRINKING FROM A VERY CLEAR STREAM. Our baby gives herself to me completely. There is no hesitation, no reservation, no holding back, no coldness, no craft, no tremor or fear in her love. Although our relationship may encompass tears, frustration, even fury, it is an utterly reliable bond. As it grows, her love is literally unadulterated. Her love is wholly of the child, pure in its essence as children are in their direct passions. Children do not love wisely, but perhaps they love the best of all.

Summer Pond

THE NEW, HUMAN-MADE POND IS A BEAU-tiful expanse of water that took us such a short time, in the scheme of things, to grow. Two years ago, it was an old field, and that is what it had been for the two centuries after it was stripped of grand white pine. The grass that grew upon it fed the flock of sheep the poorhouse indigent tended, and the cows and horses of the long succession of farmers did their best with its sloping rubble. The shoots of grass must have been eaten to the quick each summer, the ground picked over for rocks, planted some years. The land sprouted a crazy tangle of vintage fences, half-sunk concrete water troughs and the bases to vanished barns. The field went to grass, then hay, then goldenrod, asters, burdocks. Finally, one day we looked at it and we imagined water in a trough lit by sun, white birch reflected like fingers, we saw a pond.

It took two years and a lot of heavy equipment. In all stages of its making, the pond has taught us more than we expected about the woods around us. As soon as the topsoil was scraped off and piled aside for later, to be replaced like frosting on the built dikes, the killdeer arrived. They laid their eggs in shallow cups in the ground and scissored sharply through the air when anyone stepped too near. In a hiatus of excavation work, as the rains came, they raised their young and then they disappeared. The dozers returned. In the dry fall with the stream beds no more than trickles the tiny pool in the bottom of the pond attracted, from the woods, all of the inhabitants that keep themselves invisible. The fine mud held the impressions of their passage for days and allowed us to identify and record.

First there was the mysteriously large dog track which was not that of a dog at all, but the print of a coyote. Having once been eradicated from this area, coyotes seemed to have moved north and mixed to some degree with the Canadian gray wolf, before they returned in the 1970s, attracted by winter-killed deer whose numbers had grown even past those that blaze-orange clad humans could eradicate. There is now an open season on coyote here, with radio-collar hunting legal. Over the door of the local general store the stuffed head of a coyote, its tongue painted pink, snarls feebly at a line of fishing hats. They're shy creatures to begin with, and the snarl is wishful thinking on the part of a hunter. Out here, coyotes have become so preternaturally elusive that they don't dare howl. They have fallen silent, and somehow they have survived. I was delighted to see the track, for I would rather have coyotes in the woods controlling the deer herd than most of the hunters I meet gearing up with coffee and ammo and cheap licenses all November. Our windows have been blasted out by hunters, narrowly missing me once. But no coyote has ever leapt through.

Raccoons, hands delicate and spiny, waddle to the water, fat on berries and acorns. A doe, a fawn, travel down every morning. My favorite three hen turkeys gabble past occasionally. A blue heron stalks speculatively along the edge of the growing pool, and then there arrives the lone Canada goose.

Because they mate for life, this lone goose is obviously in mourning, immersed in a sumptuous sorrow. Geese in a flock are organically connected, wonderfully gregarious and of a single mind. I've seen a dozen fly down reaching for the water in formation, with precision pilots' unison, all of them landing with one brief splash. And, too, I've been among them when they massed on a northern lake to fly south. I've sat on a dock in darkness listening until I knew their language all around me was complex, spiritual. I've waited for them to rise, to take direction, until my bones grew cold. So I imagine that this lone goose is an ascetic, a bewildered mourner.

By night the great bird beds in the new-grown rye grass, by day it crops the shoots and surveys its own personal pond, now filling rapidly. We put out cracked corn, oatmeal, barley, suet, and whole grain bread. Each morning we rise in the clear air and check the goose. And there it is, day after day, its neck an abrupt black periscope. It doesn't fly, it doesn't swim, it just paces. Back and forth, along the side of the pond, it strides like any widow or widower trying to outwalk loss.

And then one day the goose is gone and the field is, too—the grass is turned inside out, into its opposite, for now where hoofed animals grazed fish rise, where dry bales were cut waves lap. Where the ground once absorbed the human glance now it gives back doubled images—dark pines in banks, an old sugarbush of ragged maples, a tiny Douglas fir that grew as a transplant from a Christmas tree, our own reflections and the butter yellow grass springing thick and sudden.

The fox

WORKING THIS AFTERNOON WITH THE DOOR open, breeze blowing through, birdsong, an occasional wasp throwing itself at the screen, I suddenly sense something different and lift my eyes without moving. A fox has crept around the corner of the building and is now posed, a long streak of rust, an exotic. The red fox was imported by homesick English settlers and it is the gray fox that is native to

New England. At any rate, this Mayflower descendant regards me through the screen. We look directly at each other—the face of a fox is exquisitely beautiful and eerily human, its eyes almond dark and slanted in the darkness of its fur, its muzzle sharp and sensitive, its tall ears flaring. I do not move, even blink, and the fox takes its time assessing me until it decides I'm furniture and then walks, unhurriedly, across the yard.

The fox sits down on the grass. It seems completely at home, indecisive, bored. Doglike, it stretches its mouth in a yawning whine, lifts a black-tipped paw and scratches languidly behind its ear. It saunters to the little dried-up streambed and then, without gathering itself in any visible way, springs high. This is a ballet leap, an upward float. The fox lands with the alacrity of a bounced ball, then hops high again.

A secret witness to grace, this moment breaks across me with a sudden fierceness. Along with the joy of our new baby and the thrills of preschoolers, we are living out the turmoil that attends both supporting and letting go of teenagers who have unfathomable behavioral problems. Michael finishes his book, *The Broken Cord*, a record of his search for the explanation of our eldest adopted son's recently diagnosed problem—Fetal Alcohol Syndrome. Though Adam suffers a variety of serious physical ailments and shows signs of poor impulse control, an inability to make abstract decisions, and attention deficit disorder, he possesses an instinct for kindness. Every afternoon he telephones out of concern. "How's it going, Ma?" he asks. "What's the baby up to?" When he's off work and with us at home he sits and holds his newest sister in a trance of mystified adoration.

For us, each day, a thousand swords hang by a thousand hairs. Michael visits counselors, begs special favors from exhausted teachers. We plead, cajole, humiliate ourselves for, and desperately love these children, hoping there will be a miracle, a change, that some form of therapy or just the craziness of attachment will heal and take them through these precarious days. So I describe the fox in its leap, a living question mark. I concentrate upon the mysterious gift in order to endure the bleak facts of our two other older children's emotional desperations. To watch a wild creature move is like a visual prayer, and when I tell about the moment to my husband, his face exhausted with our second son's cruelty, he is for a moment diverted in thought. We take long walks. Sometimes we hold hands so hard we leave nail marks in each other's palms.

An all-licorice dinner to saturate the senses

NOW, BEYOND THE LIMITS OF THE THINLY grassed yard studded with healthy golden dandelions, the ferns have unfurled to the tips. Up and down the pale deadwood of the old elm tree a pileated woodpecker bounds. The pileated, a bird precise in all of its movements, probes the tree with surgical exactitude for about fifteen minutes. Once, its armlike wings seem to clench, muscular, around a small jagged piece of branch. It drums, its head a piston blur of red, its crest vibrating. As suddenly, it launches off, a fierce, black boomerang.

I watch the pileated woodpecker thinking it looks ... it looks ... *delicious*. Not that I would ever eat a pileated woodpecker. Yet, the sight of its licorice black feathers makes me hungry. Perhaps it is just depression—this consuming urge to eat everything I see. As if intuiting my shameful secret, not three days later, as I am loudly and dramatically struggling with

work, Michael gallantly announces that he is con-
cocting an all-licorice meal. This fabulous menu
includes my favorite Ojibwa traditional food—wild
rice. The very thought of this meal still cheers me on
gloomy summer days when the hated heat springs
out of the sky early in the morning and the sun
drives down mercilessly.

All-Licorice Dinner Menu

To start with, a small blue glass of Anisette
straight from the freezer, where it has become very
cold and slightly thickened. Stir with a black licorice
swizzle.

FENNEL AND CHICORY SALAD
6 servings

Salt to taste
1 garlic clove, peeled
½ cup extra-virgin olive oil
1 tablespoon balsamic vinegar
1 tablespoon low-calorie mayonnaise
Freshly ground pepper to taste
1 head of chicory, torn into bite-size pieces

1 fennel bulb, sliced into thin strips
2 anchovy fillets, chopped fine (optional)
Pinch of dried oregano
1 teaspoon capers
1 hard-cooked egg, sliced
1 scallion, finely chopped

1. Sprinkle the bottom of a salad bowl with salt and rub it with the garlic. Add the oil, vinegar, mayonnaise, and pepper. Stir with a wooden spoon until well mixed.

2. Add remaining ingredients and toss lightly.

ANISE DUCK AND WILD RICE CASSEROLE
4 servings

One 4-pound duck, cut into quarters
2 tablespoons butter
1 cup finely chopped onion
1 clove garlic, finely minced
4 cups boiling chicken stock
Salt and freshly ground black pepper
1 cup mushrooms, coarsely chopped
1 tablespoon dried Juneberries or cherries
¾ teaspoon aniseeds, crushed

¼ teaspoon cayenne pepper
1 cup uncooked wild rice, thoroughly rinsed

1. In a skillet, brown the duck in the butter, then transfer it to a heavy Dutch oven, setting aside. Pour off most of the fat from the skillet and add the onion and garlic. Cook, stirring, until onion is transparent.

2. Add the hot stock to the skillet. Stir with a wooden spoon to dissolve the brown particles that cling to the bottom and sides of the skillet.

3. Pour the liquid over the duck and season with salt and pepper; cover. Cook for about 45 minutes over low heat, until duck begins to be tender. Remove excess fat. Add remaining ingredients, cover, and cook for an additional 40 minutes, or until the rice is al dente.

FENNEL RISOTTO
About 6 servings

1 pound sweet bulb fennel (2 to 3 bulbs,
   depending on size)
7 tablespoons butter
1 onion, thinly sliced
3 to 3¼ cups long-grain rice

10 cups boiling chicken or duck stock
Salt to taste
¾ cup grated Parmesan cheese

1. Wash the fennel bulbs thoroughly and slice thinly.

2. Melt 5 tablespoons of the butter, add the onion and fennel, and sauté gently until fennel just begins to soften.

3. Add the rice and fry until it begins to brown. Pour in a cup of boiling stock.

4. Cook over moderate heat until all the liquid has been absorbed, stirring constantly, and continue adding stock in this fashion until all has been absorbed and the rice is tender.

5. Add salt to taste. Stir in the remaining butter and the Parmesan, cover, and leave to settle for 2 to 3 minutes over low heat.

FENNEL WITH LEMON AND SPICES
4 to 6 servings

2 cups water
6 tablespoons extra-virgin olive oil
⅓ cup fresh lemon juice

Salt to taste
10 whole peppercorns
10 whole coriander seeds
2 tablespoons minced shallots
6 parsley sprigs
¼ teaspoon dried thyme
¼ teaspoon aniseeds
4 small heads of fennel

1. Combine the water, oil, lemon juice, salt, peppercorns, coriander seeds, and shallots in a large saucepan. Tie the parsley, thyme, and aniseeds in cheesecloth and add to liquid. Cover, bring to a boil, and simmer 10 minutes.

2. Trim off the top leaves and tough outer stalks of the fennel. Cut the vegetable into quarters and add to the saucepan. Cover and simmer until the fennel is tender, 30 to 40 minutes.

ANISE APPLES
6 servings

1 cup brown sugar
2 cups boiling water
½ teaspoon aniseeds

¼ *teaspoon salt*
6 *firm baking apples*

1. Combine the sugar, water, aniseeds, and salt in a 6-cup saucepan. Mix well, bring to a boil, and simmer for 5 minutes.

2. Peel, quarter, and core the apples. Drop them, two at a time, into the syrup; cover. Simmer for 10 to 12 minutes, or until fruit is tender. Lift out apples with a slotted spoon. Cool.

3. When all the apples are cooked, cook the syrup until it is thick. Pour it over apples. Serve with whipped cream and Anise Cookies (see following recipe).

ANISE COOKIES
Makes 84 small cookies

½ *cup butter, at room temperature*
1 *teaspoon baking soda*
1 *teaspoon aniseeds*
¼ *teaspoon salt*
1 *cup sugar*
1 *large egg*
2 ¼ *cups sifted all-purpose flour, plus additional*
1 *teaspoon cream of tartar*

1. Preheat oven to 350 degrees.

2. Combine the butter, soda, aniseeds, and salt. Mix well and gradually blend in the sugar. Beat in the egg. Sift the flour with cream of tartar and stir it into the batter.

3. Shape the batter into half-inch balls and place them on ungreased cookie sheets, not too close together. Dip fork tines into flour and press the fork into each cookie in a crosshatch pattern. Bake for 8 minutes. Cool on wire racks.

VERY ANISE CAKES
Makes about 24 cakes

¼ cup boiling water
2 tablespoons aniseeds
4 tablespoons Cognac or licorice schnapps
4 cups sifted flour
½ cup granulated sugar
1 cup sweet butter
About ¼ cup ice water

1. Pour boiling water over aniseeds and allow to steep in a warm place for 30 minutes. Add brandy or schnapps.

2. Combine flour and sugar in a large mixing bowl. Add butter and blend thoroughly with a pastry cutter. Slowly work in the steeped aniseeds and liquid.

3. Add enough ice water to allow the dough to stick together but not become soggy. Chill in refrigerator for 1 hour.

4. Roll out dough to ⅛-inch thickness on a lightly floured board. Cut into shapes with cookie cutter.

5. Bake on ungreased sheet at 350 degrees for 15 to 20 minutes, or until golden.

Yes, this is a heavy dose of licorice, indeed. But as with all excesses that saturate the senses, this dinner has a purifying effect upon the mind.

Art and Play

SHE HATES THE PLAYPEN AND PREFERS TO BE in the thick of things, not apart from us, even with the cleverest toys. She hates her car seat. She tolerates her baby carrier only in short bursts. Help, help, help. I spread toys in a hazard-free trajectory across the carpet laid by the marijuana grower. As I write I hear her dogged progress. This will last fifteen minutes, until she explores the last toy, a musical bluebird with an orange beak and great black cartoon eyes. She has learned how to prop herself, how to swivel on her stomach, but she can't crawl, not yet. Instead, she lunges. She props herself on her arms and pushes with her knees, lands with a solid thump, pushes up, and throws herself again and again toward the toy. It is a paradigm of something, I think, idly, pausing to study her absolute striving concentration, but what? Turning back to this page, I know. It is what I am doing now. My face is hers. Unyielding eagerness. That is her work, just as this page is my play, just as all this is our life. It is what we do, afraid and avid, full of desire, hurling ourselves again and again toward the musical object.

Bathing Children

THE STRANGE MARKS APPEAR AND MULTIPLY until our daughters are covered with itchy blotches of chicken pox. It is not a serious disease when you are still young, but our four-year-old is infuriated by the itch, so she lies in shallow oatmeal water on her

back while I pour the soothing stuff over the long,
pale, forked front of her. She's got them everywhere—in the corners of her eyes, armpits, everywhere. Yet she lies there in relief, so uncomplainingly,
so still, while I pour the water a thousand times from
the red plastic cup.

I bathe our babies every day. It's much better
than going to church. Across her thin torso, her
vividly dotted breast, the water falls—a sacrament,
the tedious repetition of a miracle. I unfold the towel
to accept her from the bath and she steps into it to be
patted dry. In a fresh gown, she comes to fall asleep
in her parents' bed. She droops anxiously into herself—it is late in the afternoon, the golden time of
animal peace. I lie against her to calm her. I do not
sleep because it is too sweet. She is a radiance. Our
hearts throb, our eyes close, her dreams well up in
her like water, and I am the screen upon which these
images fall.

Mirrors

THE BRITISH PSYCHOANALYST D. W. WINNI-
cott theorized that a mother's face becomes for a

short while an essential personal mirror that helps a baby to form a self. During these long passionate gazes, these exchanges, between mother and baby, something complex is happening. Such looking reinforces the reality of the baby's feelings. We spend hours staring into each other's eyes. Sometimes our exchange is so intense that my own face loses its habitual composure and I experience an uncanny body confusion—I feel my expression continually slipping into our baby's.

The Ojibwa word for mirror, *wabimujichagwan*, means "looking at your soul," a concept that captures some of the mystery of image and substance. If it is true that we are mirrors to our infants and that looking forms the boundaries of a self, then perhaps we are also helping to form a spiritual soul self during these concentrated love gazes during which time stops, the air dims, the earth cools, and a sense of deep rightness takes hold of our being.

WINNICOTT went still further and theorized that the companionable mirroring and self gathering that goes on helps engender one particular and special talent—the ability to be alone. To concentrate oneself, to enjoy personal solitude, is a capability formed during the creation of a self, and to have a mother who will more or less attend to needs, hold, burp, feed, change, and so on aids in forming a personality deeply comfortable with itself. I think of the image of weighted toys, untippable, bouncing upright after a blow. Perhaps even now I can help stand her upright, on her own, later on in life. Jiggling baby softly, holding her, comforting, I sometimes imagine I am sifting sand to her feet.

Rage

HOW I ADMIRE THEIR TANTRUMS, WHAT AWE! How do we lose the ability to pitch such magnificent fits? Of course, it is true that my daughters sometimes shock, embarrass, and humiliate me in public, and at those times I wish we all might sink into the earth. But that passes once we are alone, and once we are truly alone, in our house or outdoors far from neighbors, I can let their fury fly.

I secretly dote on the ferocity of our five-year-old because it is so unexpected—she is warm, a hugger, with passionate brown eyes and an artist's ready emotions. Her anger is a shock—we suddenly discover inner tempests! As long as the fury isn't aimed directly at me, I can appreciate these storms. I try to think of her rage as a force of human nature. Lightning pulses, thunder rolls low and near. She is swept along by dark inner winds. From the other side of the door to the bedroom where I have carefully led her, I hear the delivery of great pillowed blows as she pounds her bed. Her voice rises, delirious with power.

I will rage, she growls triumphantly to the walls, *I will rage.*

The Veils

IT HAS DROPPED ACROSS MY FACE AGAIN, THE white net, the cloud that at one time or another obscures the features of every woman I have known. It is a snow falling, always, between my face and your face, the shocked expression of social chastity, the charged atoms of social courtesy. Oversimplified emotion, parenthetical dreams, the message is too acute. The veil speaks possession and possessed desire. A violent grace is required, to lift the veil all on your own. By custom, the authority of touch is given to the priest, the husband. The woman's hands are always too heavy, the woman's hands are filled.

The veil is the symbol of the female hymen, and to lift it was once, and often still is, the husband's first marital privilege. The veil is the mist before the woman's face that allows her to limit her vision to the here, the now, the inch beyond her nose. It is an illusion of safety, a flimsy skin of privacy that encourages violation. The message behind the veil is touch me, I'm yours. The purity is fictional, coy. The veil is the invitation to tear it away.

Three photographs

Mary Lefavor, my grandmother—Ojibwa, French, and Scots, perhaps a descendant of the Selkirkers of Rudolph's land—stands beside a fellow first communicant. No more than ten or eleven years old, both are crowned with lilies and carnations, holding Christ's symbol erect. They are captured in the white shadow and the air of their substanceless caves, the veils they wear. My grandmother's face is beautiful, her ankles thick, her eyes too serious. It is as if, in this picture, she knows that she is about to enter a room with many doors, but no windows.

At fourteen she marries, and bears a stillborn child. More children follow—born in a log house raised on allotment land—and other women's children, too, children she loved and raised for others. A reticent woman of profound goodness.

Next photograph:

My mother on her wedding day, so beautiful with her veil thrown back she clouds my father's shy face with happiness. She is adored, the ecstasy is on her, so plain to see. She is leaving the Turtle Mountain Reservation to live with a high school teacher. Ralph Erdrich. She is leaving her mother's house. Home country. Yet there is something in her face of all that is to come—the healthy children, the long marriage, the love that is to bear the weight of conflict through so many decades, a durable look of pleasure.

Last picture:

Me at seven, and that's my mother's wedding veil cut down and tacked onto a lacy headband. I might as well be holding my grandmother's candle, too. It is exactly the same. I have made my first confession. My first sin was lying, the only sin at which I was accomplished. Now, absolved, I wear a new nylon dress that feels like a hair shirt—the bodice is small and the seams scratch underneath my arms. My bangs are curled on rags, my hair reaches down to the small of my back, and I have rehearsed over and over in air and in the mirror the act of tipping my head back, eyes shut and tongue out, receiving Christ.

The precious no

To keep my mouth shut. To turn away my face. To walk back down the aisle. To slap the bishop back when he slapped me during Confirmation. To hold the word *no* in my mouth like a gold coin, something valued, something possible. To teach the *no* to our daughters. To value their *no* more than their compliant *yes*. To celebrate *no*. To grasp the word *no* in your fist and refuse to give it up. To support the boy who says *no* to violence, the girl who will not be violated, the woman who says *no, no, no, I will not*. To love the *no*, to cherish the *no*, which is so often our first word. *No*—the means to transformation.

We are born in cauls and veils, and our lives as women are fierce and individual dances of shedding them. We are stepping higher, higher now, into the thinnest air. It takes about a decade of wild blue dancing to shed just one. If we are lucky and if we dance hard enough, will we be able to look each other in the eye, our faces clear, between us nothing but air?

And what do we do with the nets, the sails that luffed, that tangled around our feet? What do we do with the knowledge and the anger?

I see the veils twisted, knotted between us like sheets for escape. The taut material is strong when pulled and thinned to ropes between us. Primary cords. We can use the means and symbol of our long histories, as women, of emotional and intellectual incarceration. We can remove the flimsy shadows from before our faces and braid them into ropes. We can fasten the ropes between us so that if one of us slips, as we climb, as we live, there are others in the line to stand firm, to bear her up, to be her witnesses and anchors.

We are all bound, we are all in tatters, we are all the shining presence behind the net. We are all the face we're not allowed to touch. We are all in need of the ancient nourishment. And if we walk slowly without losing our connections to one another, if we wait, holding firm to the rock while our daughters approach hand over hand, if we can catch our mothers, if we hold our grandmothers, if we remember that the veil can also be the durable love between women.

Rose Nights, Summer Storms, Lists of Spiders and Literary Mothers

ONCE AGAIN MY ROSES ARE BLOOMING OUT-side the window, a tough rugosa called Therese Bugnet. Their full, glowing, pink heads droop directly outside the screen, heavy with last night's rain—their fragrance a clear, unspeakable luscious berry, sweet as thunder. The churr of wood frogs is still loud in the night. Clouds darken in the north. Storms hammer down from Quebec. The sky crackles, a cellophane sheath crumpled suddenly overhead. Gnats, bloodsucking, hairline loving, bite raw welts into our napes. On the outermost petal of the farthest blossom, I spy something black, large, and velvet. A huge spider made of plush. It is an opulent thing, its legs thick and curved, its eyes blue glowing spots. There's a screen between the two of us. Still, I am startled when it jumps. It moves with such mechanical and purposeful energy. Blossom to blossom, stuffing aphids into its jaws with thick limbs, mandibles clashing, it hunts.

When mating, these blue-eyed jumping spiders hold hands in the classic stance of either bashful lovers or wrestlers lethally balanced. If the male is not deeply vigilant and ready to leap backward as soon as he has succeeded in delicately thrusting the packet of his sperm into—what shall I call it—his lady's love chamber, she will grasp him closer, killingly, loving him to death, making a meal of him with her sudden sexually quickened appetite. To her, devouring her mate is a bit like smoking a cigarette after sex. That is why the male so tenderly clings to her hands, her tough pincers—he is trying both to make love to her and to survive her.

The example of the spider's courtship, like that of the praying mantis who cannibalizes her mate, fascinates because it seems so improbable in its contrast to our human arrangements in which men are physically the stronger and in most cases still dominate the world despite our hopeful advances, our power feminism.

Women writers live rose nights and summer storms, but like the blue-eyed jumping spider opposite our gender, must often hold their mates and families at arm's length or be devoured. We are wolf spiders, carrying our babies on our backs, and we move slowly but with more accuracy. We learn how to conserve our energy, buy time, bargain for the hours we need.

Every female writer starts out with a list of other female writers in her head. Mine includes, quite pointedly, a mother list. I collect these women in my heart and often shuffle through the little I know of their experiences to find the toughness of spirit to deal with mine.

Jane Austen—no children, no marriage. Mary Wollstonecraft—died in childbirth. Charlotte Brontë—died of hyperemesis gravidarum, a debilitating and uncontrollable morning sickness. Anne Brontë and Emily Brontë—no children or marriage. George Eliot, a.k.a. Mary Ann Evans—banned from society for an illicit liaison with a married man. No children. George Sand, Harriet Beecher Stowe, Elizabeth Gaskell—children. Emily Dickinson—no children, no marriage. Virginia Woolf—no children. Willa Cather, Jean Rhys, Djuna Barnes, Isak Dinesen—none. Kay Boyle and Meridel LeSueur—many children and political lives. Sigrid Undset, children, and Anna Akhmatova. Zora Neale Hurston, Dorothy Parker, Lillian Hellman. None. None. None. Grace Paley, Tillie Olsen—children. Toni Morrison—children. Anne Sexton. Adrienne Rich—children. Anne Tyler, Erica Jong, Alice Walker, Alice Munro, and Alice Hoffman. Children. Joan Didion. Mary

Gordon. Rosellen Brown, Robb Forman Dew, and Josephine Humphreys and Mona Simpson. Children. Isabel Allende, Jayne Anne Phillips, Linda Hogan, Sharon Olds, Louise Glück, Jane Smiley, and many, many others.

Reliable birth control is one of the best things that's happened to contemporary literature—that can be seen from the list above. Surely, slowly, women have worked for rights and worked for respect and worked for emotional self-sufficiency and worked for their own work. Still it is only now that mothers in any number have written literature. I beg a friend to send me Jane Smiley's thoughts on the subject— "Can Mothers Think?" In this piece, she speculates on writing and motherhood, upon what we do write, what we will write, how it will be different.

A mother's vision would encompass survival, she says, *would encompass the cleaning up of messes.*

A mother's vision includes tough nurturance, survival love, a demanding state of grace. It is a vision slowly forming from the body of work created by women. I imagine a wide and encompassing room filled with women lost in concentration. They are absorbed in the creation of an emotional tapestry, an intellectual quilt. Here a powerful blossom forms, there a rushing city, a river so real it flows, a slow root, a leaf. And, too, pieces that do not seem to fit into the scheme at all incorporate themselves in startling ways.

There is labor itself—birth as original a masterpiece as death. There is the delicate overlapping flower of another human personality forming before your eyes, and you blessed and frightened to be part of it. There is the strange double vision, the you and not you of a genetic half replicated in the physical body of another—your eyebrows appear, your mother's heart line, your father's crooked little finger. There is the tedious responsibility of domesticity that alternates with a hysterical sense of destined fate—the bigness and the smallness.

Writing as a mother shortly after bearing, while nurturing, an infant, one's heart is easily pierced. To look full face at evil seems impossible, and it is difficult at first to write convincingly of the mean, the murderous, the cruelty that shadows mercy and pleasure and ardor. But as one matures into a fuller grasp of the meaning of parenthood, to understand the worst becomes a crucial means of protecting the innocent. A mother's tendency to rescue fuels a writer's careful anger.

The close reexperiencing of childhood's passions and miseries, the identification with powerlessness, the apprehension of the uses of power, flow inevitably from a close relationship with a son or daughter. Perhaps most shaking, the instinct to protect becomes overwhelming. A writer's sympathies, like forced blooms, enlarge in the hothouse of an infant's need. The ability to look at social reality with an unflinching mother's eye, while at the same time guarding a helpless life, gives the best of women's work a savage coherence.

Rather than submit her child to slavery, Toni Morrison's Sethe kills her daughter, an act of ruthless mercy. The contradiction, purity, gravity of mother love pulls us all to earth.

"Too thick," says a character of Sethe's mother love, "too thick."

Sigrid Undset's extraordinary Kristin Lavransdatter, a woman whose life is shaped by powerful acts of love, commits sins unthinkable for her time and yet manages to protect her children.

"Milk brain," a friend calls these maternal deep affections that prime the intellect. Milk wisdom. Milk visions.

I exist, I simply breathe, I do nothing but live.

One day as I am holding baby and feeding her, I realize that this is exactly the state of mind and heart that so many male writers from Thomas Mann to James Joyce describe with yearning—the mystery of an epiphany, the sense of oceanic oneness, the great *yes*, the wholeness. There is also the sense of a self merged and at least temporarily erased—it is death-like. I close my eyes and see Frost's too peaceful snowy woods, but realize that this is also the most alive place I know—Blake's gratified desire. These are the dark places in the big two-hearted river, where Hemingway's Nick Adams won't cast his line, the easeful death of the self of Keats's nightingale. Perhaps we owe some of our most moving literature to men who didn't understand that they wanted to be women nursing babies.

Local Deer

THE FAT LADY THINS SUDDENLY. A NEW company of woodchucks appears. There are five, and they tumble beneath my feet, knocking against the boards of the crawl space, chewing up the raisins and apples I leave by their hole. I begin to worry that the whole house may plunge into the earth. Week after week I watch the fat pups spill into the yard, tumbling onto one another, end over end, weaving themselves into a ball of woodchucks. They play under the house, sometimes right below my feet. No matter how hard I stomp they continue to loll and dig and play. They knock into the underground gas furnace, and love the big noise. I leave sliced apples outside the door. Cracked corn. Stale bread. I spread the contents of a box of half-petrified prunes on the old wooden step. All of this they gobble down, running from below the house before I've even gone inside again. After a while they become tame as children and will approach my foot to take a peanut from the toe of my boot.

So here I sit, with a peanut on my foot, as though I'm not a writer, as though I've got nothing to do but watch these careful nuisances steal toward me one muscle at a time. I should be working because our baby is asleep, but I am too busy training woodchucks. It is late summer now, the air filled with a round clarity. I'm thinking of a sentence, businesslike, a thing I can write down, when I look up from my woodchuck.

A young buck deer is watching me.

I've never seen one here before, although they

leave their tracks, two split moons, at the edge of the field and far from the road. I've fixed No Hunting signs into the sides of the trees. I've watched. I've waited the way my father taught me to wait for deer. But New Hampshire's deer herd is about half the size of Vermont's and they are nowhere near the nuisance they are in the northeastern suburbs. Simple politics. I live in a section of the state where for the price of a license a hunter can shoot any deer, doe, or fawn. Vermont has more restrictive laws, it also has a bigger winter kill-off. Deer eat rare plants as well as boring shrubs, so I know they're a mixed blessing. It is our human fault that they're now pests in many areas. At any rate, the deer I see are an unusual presence in my hunted-down stretch of the Northeast.

The young buck stands fifteen feet away, under the old apple tree someone planted here a hundred years ago. His antlers are small, still cased in velvet. He is the bronze of dead pine needles and his eyes are black rimmed in black, still and large. His neck is limber and strong. When a car passes, he freezes, but he does not move. I don't move either. He watches me carefully and then with nervous care he reaches down and picks up a hard, green apple. His head jerks up and he looks straight at me, the apple round and whole in his teeth, like the apple in the mouth of a suckling pig.

The apple begins to vanish. His tongue extends and pushes the whole thing back into his throat. I am alarmed, suddenly, as when one of my children bites off a piece of something too large to swallow. I mentally review the Heimlich maneuver. But the apple vanishes. He reaches down for another. And then, through the wide screen door, he hears the baby shake her rattle. She has awakened and she brandishes her toy at the buck. He takes one step backward, and stands in an attitude of absolute alertness, testing the noise. The rattle spins again. He turns. He walks carefully into the trees.

DEER return until the apples are gone, a doe with the young buck. She is the same shade of russet, her wide-set ears flickering and nervous, all air and grace. I look up and she is watching me, her eyes deep-water mussels, endless and grave, purple-black. She moves from the brush. Her tail is long, a dog's tail, curved and sinuous, tipped with black. She sweeps it back and forth as she browses. I grow used to them and soon I find that the deer are there, always there, in the shadows and the shapes of other things. Invisible and obvious, gray as talc and calm as sand, the deer divide themselves from the spars and bones of trees. They make themselves whole suddenly. I am not looking, and then I am looking into their eyes.

Sleepwalkers

PERHAPS I'VE PASSED ON MY EDGY SLEEPING habits to our baby. She is a light sleeper and our presences wake her continually. She has outgrown the bassinet next to our bed—she bumps its sides rolling over, waking herself to fret. And so, for the first night since she was conceived, she sleeps more than a foot away.

First she was part of me, and then she slept curled between us. Then, a night, I don't know when, she was placed in her bassinet. Now she sleeps in the next room. For nights I wake, startled, my brain humming with abysmal exhaustion, aware only in the most atavistic way that something is wrong. It is as if in sleep I have been cut in two and suddenly I miss my other half. I am there at her cry and in the deepest hour of the night we fit together again like the pieces of a broken locket. On a cot in her little room, warming gradually under webs of afghans, we nurse, sighing, becoming more separate with every breath.

THE air is moving and the leaves are talking. Somewhere in the darkness of the stripped bed of the new pond a shrill killdeer's piping. Rumble of a car passing once, twice, silence. I am sleeping hard, rolled at an angle against my husband. In the hour of the wolf our door opens and it is our five-year-old whispering in fear—another awful dream. She creeps close and I hoist her against me. Warm, she clings tight and soon her sharp breathing falls away. The night goes on. I do not sleep because it is unbearably good to lie there, witnessing in peace the oblivion of those I love. She's calmer now, lighting into sleep soft as a moth. He is dark and solid shale reaching down through the foundation and the beams of the ground. Tonight, I am more darkness through which their two bodies have passed and fused.

Love gifts

THIS MORNING AS BABY AND I READY OUR-selves to go to work, in the rain of late summer, I lift my tall rubber boot off the porch mat. I almost put my foot onto a small olive-colored bird curled in the heel. It is dead, a love-token left by the little calico kitten I rescued from beneath the house. Rocky wears two goat bells on a red leather collar, and yet she can move without a sound. She has claimed me dispassionately, as cats do, and courts me on most days by placing a killed field mouse in my shoe, which is why I always shake them out before I put them onto my feet.

My heart sinks—I do feel it drop beneath the flood of gravity—when I draw out the small weight-less body of the female goldfinch. I think of her sitting in the house the color of her husband, and of her children, who flew off, tiny puffs of silk. I suppose in the great order of life this is a little death, but the loss of that tiny, thrilling flash of light doesn't seem to me so small.

I dig a hole for the bird under soft earth where I've just planted two pots of Chinese lanterns, but I can't put her into it. I search until I find a bracket mushroom growing like a tiny bed, high, on the haunch of the old elm tree. For days afterward I cannot bear to have the cat around me and I thrust her away—so she goes, jingling through the woods with a third bell added to her collar, a cruel, avid, merry little killer. It is wrong to harbor her small blood lusts, I think, but her delicate ferocity is seductive and her cat affection an irritating compliment. I can't part with her, at any rate. And so instead I decide to trap the great gray-green feral tomcat who slips in and out of the yard. Surely he kills far more birds, I reason, as he lives entirely by his wits and claws.

Chuck's Dad

A FERAL CAT IS A BEING OF ENTIRE STEALTH, a fascination to watch. I always think of this cat as Chuck's dad—for he is big and muscular, with the flattened ears and swagger of a heavyweight boxer. He enters the area around my writing place from time to time. He strolls to the edge of the cut grass and then crouches, creeps with abominable purpose toward the feeder with fixed eyes. If he wasn't around, maybe we'd have a real wildcat or a fisher cat. Yes, I decide, definitely, I'll remove him from his little ecological niche in these woods. An easy thought, arrogant even, difficult to carry out.

I set my live trap with dry cat food, which he steals easily the first week. The second week, I get more serious and use canned wet cat food, which he also gets, scraping it from the trip plate with such prim care that he's able to back out of the trap. I put a little grease on the hinges and try to spread the cat food smoothly as Spam onto the balanced plate. He eats well yet again. Every morning, now, I eagerly approach my trap as soon as I've settled baby and see immediately that it's empty. Frustrated, challenged, I try to think like a cat, feel cat-hungers. I concentrate. Into my mind float sardines.

Sardines! I ate them as a child. I picture my father crushing the tiny soft oiled bones onto soda crackers with the flat of his knife. I am immediately positive that there is nothing so irresistible to a cat as a sardine. As well, I think of what killed dear Chuck, that tiny greedy bit of *wonder*. Instead of putting the sardine on the trap plate I put it enticingly at the far edge of the trap. The cat must, indeed, be Chuck's father. The sardine works. When I come across the yard there he is.

House cats go primitive in fear, everyone knows. Feral cats in cringing hatred, hissing and then attacking, seem possessed by devils. The cat tries to spring at me, shrieking with bared fangs, ears flattened back and great golden eyes weirdly focused. I put the mouth of the trap at the entrance to a big wire cage, open it with a stick, prod him into the cage and wire the door shut. Pure fury erupts. He flings himself end over end. I jump back, truly shocked. I've never seen such a big amount of craziness in such small quarters—the whole cage is a blur of flying cat.

I run back to the house for the rest of the sardines and return with the can. One by one, I drop the fish down through the wire spaces into the whirl of insane movement. Nothing happens after the drop of the first sardine—it vanishes as into a piranha's river boil. With the next, the shape of the cat becomes distinguishable. Another sardine and the cat slows down to chew. By the time I've peeled back the lid of the second can, he's an actual cat and by the time those sardines are finished he is looking at me with a new speculation.

He is even huger than he looked before, and bolder, though striped just like Chuck and with Chuck's eyes. His fur is long as a Persian's, matted and tufted and lopsided like a person just rising from a long sleep. He's one big bad hairdo with eyes staring out. He's not so evil, after all. Another can of sardines and I drag his cage over to a shade tree and push between the wire slats a plate of water, a cup of cream. Before I turn my back he's vacuumed the cream up. I let him be—he seems a little drunk, stunned by pleasure. I return one hour later. I would swear he's waiting for me.

Over the course of several days and many cream pots and cans of sardines, an amazing transformation takes place in the personality of this cat. I think of all the comforts cats like and offer them. On the second day, I use a twig to reach down through the wire and run the stick along his back, up and down, back and forth. He glares killingly at the stick and then, at the touch, his shoulders arch and his back stretches and he lets the stick scratch him until he's practically in tears. By the end of day three, this cat is sweet on everybody. He rubs along the sides of the cage when we come near. On day four I hear, rumbling from his chest in spurts and jets and spits like a small, rusty, outboard motor, the sound of his purr.

Francis, we call him, our greatest success in the cat rehabilitation program. A neighbor with a mouse-ridden horse barn and a milk cow falls in love with Francis and he leaves us to lead a happy, fulfilled, creamy, useful life.

Disturbances

THE CAT AND THE BLUE JAY ARE NOT SO DIF-ferent. Though the blue jay is not exactly tame, humans are responsible for the ease with which the bird has proliferated in suburban and disturbed rural country. The blue jay is an opportunist, and opportunists are survivors in every sense. They are adaptable, clever, and unprincipled. Blue jays rob the nests of songbirds, devour their eggs, pluck food from the hands of tiny children, dive-bomb other birds, scream piercingly at cats or humans who approach their nests, attack with sharp beaks. Unlike shy, solitary creatures with more refined needs, blue jays have little difficulty moving into the human world and they hold their own in common with raccoons, skunks, sparrows, ravens, grackles, starlings. And feral cats, too.

Blue jays can live in chopped-up, murdered woods, in dump lots, fancy gardens, and city boulevards. They can live in old pines and brand-new Lombardy poplars. They eat dropped lunch, seeds, apple cores, frogs, bugs, rodents, and day-flying bats. The only time they fall silent, ever, is when they've got a nest to hide. Otherwise they are obnoxiously loud. They are robber birds, *diindiisi* in Ojibwa. To the Salish Kootenai they are a mystical bird and source of medicine power. A Yurok story tells of a jealous female blue jay who put her clitoris on her head in a fit of fury. Blue jays are stubborn. They mob owls, scream convincingly as hawks. I feel more affinity for the shy thrush, the reclusive white-breasted nuthatch, the indigo bunting with its feathers of heart-breaking cerulean blue, and yet, there is something about blue jays that both delights and irritates. Audacity thrills, even from the most exasperating source.

All Mothers

I SEE MYSELF FROZEN IN A CLUTCH OF mothers, in a flock, a panic of mothers, in a spongy-shoed group who manage all of the trivia of mother-hood—the skills and lessons that must be learned, the clothes stitched and bruises kissed—with seemingly greater ease than I ever achieve. The truth is, I like doing these small things, up to a point, but when the sludge of incremental necessities becomes suffocating, I rebel and let the details slide. How glad I am to know that I am not the only one. From outside, the mothers in brilliant parkas look affable and competent, but as I sit talking among them I come to know that we are all struggling, with more or less grace, to hold on to the tiger tail of children's, husband's, parents', and siblings' lives while at the same time saving a little core of self in our own, just enough to live by.

In talking to other women over years, I begin to absorb them somehow, as if we're all permeable. Some days I'm made up of a thousand mothers who have given one ironic look, one laugh at the right moment, one exasperated wave, one acknowledgment. Mothering is a subtle art whose rhythm we collect and learn, as much from one another as by instinct. Taking shape, we shape each other, with subtle pressures and sudden knocks. The challenges shape us, approvals refine, the wear and tear of small abrasions transform until we're slowly made up of one another and yet wholly ourselves.

Women without children are also the best of mothers, often, with the patience, interest, and saving grace that the constant relationship with children cannot always sustain. I come to crave our talk and our daughters gain precious aunts. Women who are not mothering their own children have the clarity and focus to see deeply into the character of children webbed by family. A child is fortunate who feels witnessed as a person, outside relationships with parents, by another adult.

A Recidivist

FRANCIS, THE CAT WITH THE PERFECT LIFE, vanishes from his show barn and saunters, wild again, into his old haunt around my writing place. At first, he's a dark mystery. I return late from town with a precious egg salad sandwich, made fresh, just the right amount of onion and mayonnaise and pepper. I know because I've had one bite. It is a deep night, moonless, and I walk into the house leaving the car door open, dragging in the other groceries sack by sack. I'm distracted, and fifteen minutes elapse before I remember my sandwich on the dashboard. I find only the waxed paper, bitten through in a circle, unfolded by ravenous licks. Just as I reach for the paper there is an animal thump in the dark, out of sight, paws hitting earth.

The next day I'm watching a woodpecker upside down on a block of suet when the air blurs. I see the cat only as a flourish of unusual movement. Then he stops, and it is Francis. I step to the screen door, where he knows I am, and he gives me a long assessing cat stare over his shoulder. He's still fat from the cream cow and my egg salad sandwich, and he's out of practice, he has missed the woodpecker by a dog's length. He pads into a bank of cinnamon fern and nettle where I won't follow. He waits there. He's waiting for my woodpecker.

It is much harder to catch a feral cat the second time around, especially one who has chosen freedom over a life of ease, a hard-core tomcat like Francis. I rush immediately to set up the trap with sardines, but he now associates them with captivity and avoids the whole contraption in contempt. I try liverwurst, salmon skins, Fancy Feast, and finally, egg salad.

What a sucker! I gloat over Francis the next day as he cringes in the cage, hissing, but with very little conviction. I have the sense that this is all pro forma, that Francis is kidding with me, playing around at being wild this time, and sure enough it only takes a day to make him croon beneath my hands. I don't know what to do with Francis, though. He's obviously fueled by cat desires, cat testosterone, and prefers to be a feral predator. If I had him neutered, he would cleave to the side of his cream cow instead of waiting in the shadows to lure out the summer-people's meek-eyed female cats, and eat my wood-peckers. He would get old and fat on mice instead of challenging the inevitable stronger tomcat, instead of being chased from farmyards with firecrackers, pep-pered with bird shot.

I lock Francis in the lean-to and decide, that evening, that I'll bring him to the vet in the morning. It is the right, the responsible, the correct thing to do as a good citizen, but Francis does not agree.

He is gone, through an old skunk tunnel or a crack in the boards so thin I can't believe he could squeeze through. He is gone and this time nothing—not egg salad, not canned mackerel, not even Polish sausage—will lure him back.

PART IV

Fall

Skunk Dreams

WHEN I WAS FOURTEEN, I SLEPT ALONE ON a North Dakota football field under cold stars on an early September night. Fall progresses swiftly in the Red River Valley, and I happened to hit a night when frost formed in the grass. A skunk trailed a plume of steam across the forty-yard line near moonrise. I tucked the top of my sleeping bag over my head and was just dozing off when the skunk walked onto me with simple authority.

Its ripe odor must have dissipated in the heavy summer grass and ditch weeds, because it didn't smell all that bad, or perhaps it was just that I took shallow breaths in numb surprise. I felt him, her, whatever, pause on the side of my hip and turn around twice before evidently deciding I was a good place to sleep. At the back of my knees, on the quilting of my sleeping bag, it trod out a spot for itself and then, with a serene little groan, curled up and lay perfectly still. That made two of us. I was wildly awake, trying to forget the sharpness and number of skunk teeth, trying not to think of the high percentage of skunks with rabies, or the reason that on camping trips my father always kept a hatchet underneath his pillow.

Inside the bag, I felt as if I might smother. Carefully, making only the slightest of rustles, I drew the bag away from my face and took a deep breath of the night air, enriched with skunk, but clear and watery and cold. It wasn't so bad, and the skunk didn't stir at all, so I watched the moon—caught that night in an envelope of silk, a mist—pass over my sleeping field of teenage guts and glory. The grass harbored a sere dust both old and fresh. I smelled the heat of spent growth beneath the rank tone of my bag-mate—the stiff fragrance of damp earth and the thick pungency of newly manured fields a mile or two away—along with my sleeping bag's smell, slightly mildewed, forever smoky. The skunk settled even closer and began to breathe rapidly; its feet jerked a little like a dog's. I sank against the earth, and fell asleep too.

Of what easily tipped cans, what molten sludge, what dogs in yards on chains, what leftover macaroni casseroles, what cellar holes, crawl spaces, burrows taken from meek woodchucks, of what miracles of garbage did my skunk dream? Or did it, since we can't be sure, dream the plot of *Moby-Dick*, how to properly age Parmesan, or how to restore the brick-walled tumble-down creamery that was its home? We don't know about the dreams of any other biota, and even much about our own. If dreams are an actual dimension, as some assert, then the usual rules of life by which we abide do not apply. In that place, skunks may certainly dream themselves into the vests of stockbrokers. Perhaps that night the skunk and I dreamed each other's thoughts or are still dreaming them. To paraphrase the problem of the Taoist philosopher Chuang Tzu, I may be a woman who has dreamed herself a skunk, or a skunk still dreaming that she is a woman.

In a book called *Death and Consciousness*, David H. Lund—who wants very much to believe in life after death—describes human dream life as a possible model for a disembodied existence.

"Many of one's dreams," he says, "are such that they involve the activities of an apparently embodied person whom one takes to be oneself as long as one dreams. . . . Whatever is the source of the imagery . . . apparently has the capacity to bring about images of a human body and to impart the feeling that the body is mine. It is, of course, just an image body, but it serves as a perfectly good body for the dream experience. I regard it as mine, I act on the dream environment by means of it, and it constitutes the center of the perceptual world of my dream."

OVER the years I have acquired and reshuffled my beliefs and doubts about whether we live on after death—in any shape or form, that is, besides the molecular level at which I am to be absorbed by the taproots of cemetery elms or pines and the tangled mats of fearfully poisoned, too green lawn grass. I want something of the self on whom I have worked so hard to survive the loss of the body (which, incidentally, the self has done a fairly decent job of looking after, excepting spells of too much cabernet and a few idiotic years of rolling my own cigarettes out of Virginia Blond tobacco). I am put out with the marvelous discoveries of the intricate biochemical configuration of our brains, though I realize that the processes themselves are quite miraculous. I understand that I should be self-proud, content to gee-whiz at the fact that I am the world's only mechanism that can admire itself. I should be grateful that life is here today, though gone tomorrow, but I can't help it. I want more.

*   *   *

SKUNKS don't mind each other's vile perfume. Obviously, they find each other more than tolerable. And even I, who have been in the presence of a direct skunk hit, wouldn't classify their weapon as mere smell. It is more on the order of a reality-enhancing experience. It's not so pleasant as standing in a grove of old-growth cedars, or on a lyrical moonshed plain, or watching trout rise to the shadow of your hand on the placid surface of an Alpine lake. When the skunk lets go, you're surrounded by skunk presence: inhabited, owned, involved with something you can only describe as powerfully *there*.

I woke at dawn, stunned into that sprayed state of being. The dog that had approached me was rolling in the grass, half addled, sprayed too. My skunk was gone. I abandoned my sleeping bag and started home. Up Eighth Street, past the tiny blue and pink houses, past my grade school, past all the addresses where I baby-sat, I walked in my own strange wind. The streets were wide and empty; I met no one—not a dog, not a squirrel, not even an early robin. Perhaps they had all scattered before me, blocks away. I had gone out to sleep on the football field because I was afflicted with a sadness I had to dramatize. Mood swings had begun, hormones, feverish and raw. They were nothing to me now. My emotions had seemed vast, dark, and sickeningly private. But they were minor, mere wisps, compared to skunk.

A short personal dream history. The fence.

I HAVE FOUND THAT MY BEST DREAMS COME to me in cheap motels. One such dream about an especially haunting place occurred in a rattling room in Valley City, North Dakota. There, in the home of the Winter Show, in the old Rudolph Hotel, I was to spend a week-long residency as a poet-in-the-schools. I was supporting myself, at the time, by teaching poetry to children, convicts, rehabilitation patients, high school hoods, and recovering alcoholics. What a marvelous job it was, and what opportunities I had to dream, since I paid my own lodging and lived low, sometimes taking rooms for less than ten dollars a night in motels that had already been closed by local health departments.

The images that assailed me in Valley City came about because the bedspread was so thin and worn—a mere brown tissuey curtain—that I had to sleep beneath my faux-fur Salvation Army coat, wearing all of my clothing, even a scarf. Cold often brings on the most spectacular of dreams, as though the brain has been incited to fevered activity. On that particular frigid night, the cold somehow seemed to snap boundaries, shift my time continuum, and perhaps even allow me to visit my own life in a future moment. After waking once, transferring the contents of my entire suitcase onto my person, and shivering to sleep again, I dreamed of a vast, dark, fenced place. The fencing was chain-link in places, chicken wire, sagging X wire, barbed wire on top, jerry-built with tipped-out poles and uncertain corners nailed to log posts and growing trees. And yet it was quite impermeable and solid, as time-tested, broken-looking things so often are.

Behind it, trees ran for miles—large trees, grown trees, big pines the likes of which do not exist on the Great Plains. In my dream I walked up to the fence, looked within, and saw tawny, humpbacked elk move among the great trunks and slashing green arms. Suave, imponderable, magnificently dumb, they lurched and floated through the dim-complexioned air. One turned, however, before they all vanished, and from either side of that flimsy-looking

barrier there passed between us a look, a commu-
nion, a long and measureless regard that left me, on
waking, with a sensation of penetrating sorrow.

The woman pine. The dream fence.

I DON'T THINK ABOUT MY DREAM FOR MANY
years, until after I move to New Hampshire. I have
become civilized and sedentary since the days when I
slept with skunks, and I've turned inward. Unused to
walking in the woods, at first I do not even realize
that trees drop branches—often large ones—or that
there is any possible danger in going out on windy
days, drawn by the natural drama. There is a white
pine I love, a tree of the size foresters call overgrown,
a waste, a thing made of long-since harvestable material. The tree is so big that three people can barely
reach around it. Standing at the bottom, craning back,
fingers clenched in grooves of bark, I hold on as the
crown of the tree roars and beats the air a hundred
feet above. The movement is frantic, the soft-needled
branches long and supple, I think of a woman tossing,
anchored in passion: calm one instant, full-throated
the next, hair vast and dark, shedding the piercing,

fresh oil of broken needles. I go to visit her often, and walk onward, farther, though it is not so far at all, and then one day I reach the fence.

Chain-link in places, chicken wire, sagging X wire, barbed wire on top, jerry-built with tipped-out poles and uncertain corners nailed to log posts and growing trees, still it seems impermeable and solid. Behind it, there are trees for miles: large trees, grown trees, big pines. I walk up to the fence, look within, and can see elk moving. Suave, imponderable, magnificently dumb, they lurch and float through the dim air.

I am on the edge of a game park, a rich man's huge wilderness, probably the largest parcel of protected land in western New Hampshire, certainly the largest privately owned piece I know about. At forty square miles—more than 25,000 acres—it is bigger than my mother's home reservation. And it has the oddest fence around it that I've ever seen, the longest and the tackiest. Though partially electrified, the side closest to our house is so piddling that an elk could easily toss it apart. Certainly a half-ton wild boar, the condensed and living version of a tank, could stroll right through. But then animals, much like most humans, don't charge through fences unless they have sound reasons. As I soon find out, because I naturally grow fascinated with the place, there are many more animals trying to get into the park than out, and they couldn't care less about ending up in a hunter's stew pot.

These are not wild animals, the elk—since they are grained at feeding stations, how can they be? They are not domesticated either, however, for beyond the no-hunt boundaries they flee and vanish. They are game. Since there is no sport in shooting feedlot steers, these animals—still harboring wild traits and therefore more challenging to kill—are maintained to provide blood pleasure for the members of the Blue Mountain Forest Association.

As I walk away from the fence that day, I am of two minds about the place—and I am still. Shooting animals inside fences, no matter how big the area they have to hide in, seems abominable and silly. And yet, I am glad for that wilderness. Though secretly managed and off limits to me, it is the source of flocks of evening grosbeaks and pine siskins, of wild turkeys, ravens, pileated woodpeckers, and grouse, vireo, of Eastern coyotes, oxygen-rich air, foxes, goldfinches, skunks, and bears that tunnel in and out.

I dreamed of this place in Valley City, or it

dreamed me. There is an affinity here, beyond any explanation I can offer, so I don't try. I continue to visit the tracts of big trees, and on deep nights—windy nights, especially when it storms—I like to fall asleep imagining details. I see the great crowns touching, hear the raving sound of wind and thriving, knocking cries as the blackest of ravens fling themselves across acres upon indifferent acres of tossing, old-growth pine. I fall asleep picturing how, below that dark air, taproots thrust into a deeper blankness, drinking the powerful rain.

OR IS IT so only in my dreams? The park, known locally as Corbin's Park, after its founder Austin Corbin, is knit together of land and farmsteads he bought in the late nineteenth century from 275 individuals. Among the first animals released there, before the place became a hunting club, were thirty buffalo, remnants of the vast western herds. Their presence piqued the interest of Ernest Harold Bayne, a conservation-minded local journalist, who attempted to break a pair of buffalo calves to the yoke. He exhibited them at county fairs and even knit mittens out of buffalo wool, hoping to persuade the skeptical of their usefulness. His work inspired sympathy, if not a trend for buffalo yarn, and collective zeal for the salvation of the buffalo grew so that by 1915 the American Bison Society, of which Bayne was secretary, had helped form government reserves that eventually more than doubled the herds that remained.

The buffalo dream seems to have been the park's most noble hour. Since that time it has been the haunt of wealthy hunting enthusiasts. The owner of Ruger Arms currently inhabits the stunning, butter yellow original Corbin mansion and would like to buy the whole park for his exclusive use, or so local gossip has it.

Obstacles and desire

FOR SOME MONTHS I WALK THE BOUNDARY admiring the tangled landscape, at least all that I, or baby and I, can see. She comes with me most days in her blue backpack with the aluminum frame. The walking lulls her. I feel her head settle on my back, her weight go from lively to inert. After my first apprehension and discovery, I ignore the fence. I walk along it as if it simply does not exist, as if I really am part of that place just beyond my reach.

The British psychotherapist Adam Phillips has examined obstacles from several different angles, attempting to define their emotional use. "It is impossible to imagine desire without obstacles," he writes, "and wherever we find something to be an obstacle we are at the same time desiring something. It is part of the fascination of the Oedipus story in particular, and perhaps narrative in general, that we and the heroes and heroines of our fiction never know whether obstacles create desire or desire creates obstacles." He goes on to characterize the unconscious, our dream world, as a place without obstacles: "A good question to ask of a dream is: What are the obstacles that have been removed to make this extraordinary scene possible?"

My current dream, however, is about obstacles still in place. The fence is the main component, the defining characteristic of the forbidden territory that I watch but cannot enter or experience. The obstacles that we overcome define us. We are composed of hurdles we set up to pace our headlong needs, to control our desires, or against which to measure our growth. "Without obstacles," Phillips writes, "the notion of development is inconceivable. There would be nothing to master."

Walking along the boundary of the park no longer satisfies me. The preciousness and deceptive stability of that fence begins to rankle. Longing fills me. I want to brush against the old pine bark and pass beyond the ridge, to see specifically what is there: what blue mountain, what empty views, what lavender hillside, what old cellar holes, what unlikely animals. I am filled with poacher's lust, except I want only to smell the air. The linked web restraining me begins to grate, and I start to look for weak spots, holes, places where the rough wire sags. From the moment I begin to see the fence as permeable, it is no longer a fence. I return time after time—partly to see if I can spot anyone on the other side, partly because I know I must trespass.

Then, one clear morning, while Michael is taking care of our baby, I walk alone. I travel along the fence until I come to a place that looks shaky—and is. I go through. There are no trails that I can see, and I know I need to stay away from any perimeter roads or snowmobile paths, as well as from the feeding stations where the animals congregate. I want to see the animals, but only from a distance. Of course, as I walk on, leaving a trail easily backtracked, I encounter no animals at all. Still, the terrain is beautiful, the columns of pine tall, virgin, and second growth, the patches of oak and elderly maple from an occasional farmstead knotted and patient. I am satisfied and I decide to turn back and head toward the fence again. Skirting a low, boggy area that teems with wild turkey tracks, heading toward the edge of a deadfall of trashed branches and brush, I stare too hard into the sun, and stumble.

In a half crouch, I look straight into the face of a boar, massive as a boulder. Corn-fed, razor-tusked, alert, sensitive ears pricked, it edges slightly backward into the convening shadows. Two ice picks of light gleam from its shrouded, tiny eyes, impossible to read. Beyond the rock of its shoulder, I see more: a sow and three well-grown cinnamon brown farrows crossing a small field lit by dazzling sun. The young skitter along, lumps of muscled fat on tiny hooves. They remind me of snowsuited toddlers on new skates. When they are out of sight the boar melts through the brush after them, leaving not a snapped twig or crushed leaf in his wake.

I almost don't breathe in the silence, letting the fact of that presence settle before I retrace my own tracks.

*   *   *

NEXT time, I go to the game park via front gates, driven by a friend down the avenues of tough old trees. I see herds of wild pigs and elk meandering past the residence of the gamekeeper. A no-hunting zone exists around the house, where the animals are almost tame. But I've been told by privileged hunters that just beyond that invisible boundary they vanish, becoming suddenly and preternaturally elusive.

SO WHAT is wild? What is wilderness? What are dreams but an internal wilderness and what is desire but a wildness of the soul?

THERE is something in me that resists the notion of fair use of this land if the only alternative is to have it cut up, sold off in lots, condominiumized. I like to have it *there*. Yet the dumb fervor of the place depresses me—the wilderness locked up and managed but not for its sake, the animals imported and cultivated to give pleasure through their deaths. All animals, that is, except for skunks.

Not worth hunting, inedible except to old trappers like my uncle Ben Gourneau, who boiled his skunk with onions in three changes of water, skunks pass in and out of Corbin's Park without hindrance, without concern. They live off the corn in the feeding cribs (or the mice it draws), off the garbage of my rural neighbors, off bugs and frogs and grubs. They nudge their way onto our back porch for cat food, and even when disturbed they do not, ever, hurry. It's easy to get near a skunk, even to capture one. When skunks become a nuisance, people either shoot them or catch them in crates, cardboard boxes, Havahart traps, plastic garbage barrels.

Natives of the upper Connecticut River Valley have neatly solved the problem of what to do with such catches. They hoist their trapped mustelid into the back of a pickup truck and cart the animal across the river to the neighboring state—New Hampshire to Vermont, Vermont to New Hampshire—before releasing it. The skunk population is estimated as about even on both sides.

IF I WERE an animal, I'd choose to be a skunk: live fearlessly, eat anything, gestate my young in just two months, and fall into a state of dreaming torpor when the cold bit hard. Wherever I went, I'd leave my sloppy tracks. I wouldn't walk so much as putter, destinationless, in a serene belligerence—past hunters, past death overhead, past death all around.

Fall Rains

I HAVE NO PROFOUND REASON TO BE depressed and have always hated and despised depression, fought it with every argument I can invent, tried my best to walk it off, run it off, drink it out, crush it with leaves and solitude on the Plains or in the accepting Northeastern woods. But the deaths of three of my grandparents, within months of one another, seem to trigger a downward trend I cannot stave off even with a baby in my arms. Somehow, over all these miles, I must have been sustained by my grandparents even more than I knew, because the silence in their wake roars over me, their absences shake me, and it seems as though something within me is pulled deeply under, into the earth, as though I still follow after them, stumbling, unable to say good-bye.

My maternal grandfather, Patrick Gourneau, former tribal chairman, powwow dancer, a man of subtle humor and intelligence, dies after years of wandering in a dark place. His illness was cruel and took nearly two decades to destroy him. He disappeared cell by cell, losing his sense of time and place slowly, and then weakening still further, so there was no clear moment of obvious loss, but only the tepid winding down, the tiny and incremental lacks, the odd habits becoming completely irrational, then frightening. At last, he was a paralyzed vacuity nursed with tenderness and patient irony by my grandmother. She gave to him the vigor of her old age as she had given herself to him in marriage at age fourteen—completely and with some unknown and rocklike composition of will.

Grandpa stopped recognizing me years ago, and yet, I still need to let go. Michael takes care of our home and other children, but I bring our baby along. Car seat cradled on my hip, she and I navigate airports and rental car agencies and tiny windswept hotels, traveling in the mouth of a North Dakota blizzard to the Turtle Mountain Reservation. We pull into the yard of Saint Ann's Church just as the last hymns are being sung, just as the relatives, our cousins and uncles and aunts, my mother and sister, come walking out. There is the ritual of burial, blue carnations, red-black roses, reconciliations and then a long feast, an air of terror and relief. The graves of Ojibwa, Cree, and Michif Catholics, guarded by statues of cast concrete and plastic, march up a windy hill. Our Catholic great-great-grandparents are buried behind the church, and the pagans, the traditionals, lie in yet another graveyard, where the uneven markers are crowded by sage and wild prairie rose.

The depth of his loss seems almost out of proportion, for isn't it—as most people say—a blessing? And yet, as the old go walking into night, we lose our sense of time's extension, we lose our witnesses, our living memories. We lose them and we lose the farthest reach of ourselves.

The voice in which my grandfather spoke to me is, however, laced unfathomably through the mechanism of my own brain, so that I hear him speak in clear tones. The words themselves, the meanings, are indistinguishable from the rush of wind.

Grandpa's prayer

ONE OF THE LAST FEW TIMES I STAYED WITH my grandparents, when he was well, he walked to the edge of the woods and began to pray in my presence.

I couldn't understand him because he was praying in fluid Ojibwa, a language that sounds like water hitting the bottom of a boat. He was asking the Manitous for assistance. So I sat on the wooden steps and said nothing. After a while, he turned and walked back, past his rhubarb patch. He was carrying a leather-covered bone in his hand, a prayer-bone, the hollowed foreleg of a deer into which he'd poured seeds, earth, all that he felt necessary to life. In the same way that he had prayed for a safe Apollo 11 moon landing, he told me that he had prayed for me to become famous in school. By famous, he just meant successful. He didn't mean that I should really become well-known.

The sun was coming out from under rain clouds, a golden kind of light, intensely flooding us. He wore old baggy jeans, leather boots, a green Sears work shirt and a white T-shirt under it. His hair was parted on the side and the comb tracks were still fresh. He wore glasses. One eye had crossed the last time he had a stroke. He could eat no salt, no jam. His gold tooth shone softly and his eyes were full of pleasure. I went up to my grandfather and took his arm to walk back to the house with him. There was no end to his kindness, no end to the things only he could know. I wished that he would never have to die, or lose his mind, as was happening to him slowly.

NOW, leaving his road, I begin to sing an old mocking song he taught to me and to other grandchildren, a song about old women who gossip endlessly all spring, but who love their daughters. Some Ojibwa people fear the owl, *kokoko*, but my grandfather kept an owl as a pet for many years, when my mother was a girl. She tells me that it lived in the barn, flew in and out, and walked the roof at night, hunting.

On the road to Grand Forks, baby drifting to sleep in her car seat, we quickly reach the reservation boundary. Just as we cross, I see a great gray owl roosting on a post near the highway. As we pass, the bird springs up on razored claws, silent feathers, and with four wing beats disappears into the lowering sky.

Driving slick roads

YOU CAN BE MARRIED TO THE MOST WON-derful man on earth. You're still a woman. You can be married to the Blessed Virgin. You can be married to the Pope. You can be ass-deep in money, charged with success like a brand-new car battery. You can have fifteen-minute labors and perfect breasts and you're still a woman. You're still a woman on a dogsled, in a jet. You're still a woman no matter what excuse you've given men. Can't get around it. Change your hair, kill your yeast off, and shut your eyes. You're still a woman.

I am driving the rain-punished road with sleet in my face when this sense of my sex, an overwhelming consciousness of the simple fact of my femaleness, assails me. I steer the wheel to one side a little, correcting for someone else's rutted skid. I check into my body, as into a new motel room. Carefully, I examine my structure. My hips are heavy in the cup of my seat, solid with life. My face feels simple and wide and remote from the rest of me. My eyelids prickle for sleep. With each breath, the aluminum bands in my chest tighten and relax. My shoulders must be shrugged down—they ride up when I'm nervous. I yawn, and the insides of my ears open, refreshed, curious. My hands are flexed on the wheel and my foot works brake and accelerator in slow, deliberate pumps at every turn.

The body I inhabit is gracious, a merciful shelter,

and to it I am suddenly and obscurely thankful. Again, I feel now, I am being forgiven. I have pressed the limits of its endurance. I have traveled with this body like a bird in a suitcase. I have stuffed this body with Chee-tos, then starved it like a cruel stepmother in a fairy tale. I have weakened this body by ignoring it like a dog waiting to be walked. I have pushed this body to every physical extreme I can think of—run it to a quiet halt, deranged it with poisons, sent it off on bleak sexual quests, and now forced it to make more bodies in a random paging of its DNA. After bearing a child, the body takes a generous year and even two to heal into its balance and right discretion once more. I can feel it happening, as I drive along, right here.

Now, I promise, as I do every night, that I will lay this body down gently like an animal as soon as possible. I will turn down the phone's ring, dim the lights, and shut the door.

When every inch of the world is known, sleep may be the only wilderness that we have left. In sleep's preserve, the body repairs itself, talks to itself, leads a separate life we cannot know. In dreams, our brains endlessly argue and converse. Some days, when my body wakes, it seems wiser than the consciousness that inhabits it. Unhampered by the beams of my thoughts, it performs its necessary tasks and by morning usually manages to have accomplished an active rest. While I am not there to impede its work, my body takes lessons on how to save me.

Breathe! Circulate!

Bone, muscles, cardiac cells, neurons, tissues—all are knitted together into a temporary and random genetic formation. My body knows and yet accepts its own surprises. Understanding that its span is swift, it attempts with the most diligent and touching innocence to carry along its coded text, to survive street crossings, carcinogenic junk foods, diseases, thrills of physical despair.

If, as I suspect, my body survives by uttering itself over and over again, then I have some questions. If am one word, so are my daughters, so are all of us in strings and loops. Each life is one short word slowly uttered. Again, the stone lips part. Body, what is the meaning of this absurd and complicated story? What word will be erased with me? And tell me, when you've done as you wish, when you've dragged my message from one oblivion into the next, from birth to death, who will be there to receive the burning paper? Who will uncrumple and brush away the charred edges, the washed hair, the lover's earthen touch? Who will read this female body?

The Zero

SHE SITS ON MY LAP AND LOOKS AT FIRST snow. It is not like her to be so still. Perhaps she watches my pen as it moves, a black shape, or my hand, shadowing the page. She watches the wind turn silver, the snowflakes blown backward, the sight of pure falling. We sit in the willow rocker before the window. This is a house of ardor and affection, the house of a writer, of a woman and a child—where the unborn baby stirred, the newborn nursed herself to sleep, the infant ran a plump and capable small hand through the new six-month hair, the longer nine-month hair, and now the year's growth, so fine and brown. It is a house where a child woke and pushed herself up to glare through the mesh of her bed at her mother and then, piecing together the scraps of vision through the squares, burst into a smile of astonished recognition.

I assemble the pieces to form her, too. Our children come from the house of the unborn, from the biological zero. I sit here pondering this very ordinary mystery. We do not ask for life. Our gift is our burden, and our burden is our freedom. We are free at any time to lay it down, to return to the zero, as the man who once sat in this little house did, choosing his way over what he must have seen in front of him: this view of stilled trees.

The Blue Jay's Dance

THE HAWK SWEEPS OVER, LIGHT SHINING through her rust red tail. She makes an immaculate cross in flight, her shadow running along the ground behind her as I'm walking below. Our shadows join, momentarily, and then separate, both to our appointed rounds. Always, she hunts flying into the cast of the sun, making a pass east to west. Once inside, I settle baby, resettle baby, settle and resettle myself, and have just lowered my head into my hands to proofread a page when a blur outside my vision causes me to look up.

The hawk drops headfirst out of a cloud. She folds her wings hard against her and plunges into the low branches of the apple tree, moving at such dazzling speed I can barely follow. She strikes at one of the seven blue jays who make up the raucous gang, and it tumbles before her, head over feet, end over end. She plunges after it from the branches, flops in the sun. They both light on the ground and square off, about a foot apart in the snow.

The struck jay thrusts out its head, screams, raises its wings, and dances *toward* the gray hawk. The plain of snow must seem endless, an arena without shelter, and the bird gets no help from the other six jays except loud encouragement at a safe distance. I hardly breathe. The hawk, on the ground, its wings clattering against the packed crust, is so much larger than its shadow, which has long brushed in and out of mine. It screams back, eyes filled with yellow light. Its hooked beak opens and it feints with its neck. Yet the jay, ridiculous, continues to dance, hopping forward, hornpiping up and down with tiny leaps, all of its feathers on end to increase its size. Its crest is sharp, its beak open in a continual shriek, its eye-mask fierce. It pedals its feet in the air. The hawk steps backward. She seems confused, cocks her head, and does not snap the blue jay's neck. She watches. Although I know nothing of the hawk and cannot imagine what moves her, it does seem to me that she is fascinated, that she puzzles at the absurd display before she raises her wings and lifts off.

PAST the gray moralizing and the fierce Roman Catholic embrace of suffering and fate that so often clouds the subject of suicide, there is the blue jay's dance. Beyond the impossible corners, stark cliffs, dark wells of trapped longing, there is that manic, successful jig—cocky, exuberant, entirely a bluff, a joke. That dance makes me clench down hard on life. But it is also a dance that in other circumstances might lead me, you, anyone, to choose a voluntary death. I see in that small bird's crazy courage some of what it took for my grandparents to live out the tough times. I peer around me, stroke my own skin, look into this baby's eyes that register me as a blurred self-extension, as a function of her will. I have made a pact with life: if I were to die now it would be a form of suicide for her. Since the two of us are still in the process of differentiating, since my acts are hers and I do not even think, yet, where I stop for her or where her needs, exactly, begin, I must dance for her. I must be the one to dip and twirl in the cold glare and I must teach her, as she grows, the unlikely steps.

Outwalking Death

WE PASS OUT OF THIS WORLD AS GRASSHOP-pers, the prophet Esdras complained to God, and our life is astonishment and fear. The snow is covered with a heavy crust of ice, the world seems lifeless, monotonous. The air is the gray color of the ground. Just months after our last trip to North Dakota, my father's mother, my grandmother, is dying in a far-away Minnesota hospital. Tomorrow I'll be on another plane. She has come back from the brink of death twice before and survived falls, widowhood, disease, disappointment. She has seemed so strong willed that nothing could kill her, but this is conges-tive failure of the heart.

TO WALK off the panic I feel at our impending loss, I put baby in her blue backpack and take to the snowmobile trails on a Sunday afternoon. My boots are a windfall from a friend long disappeared into the catering business. They were too big for her, just

THE BLUE JAY'S DANCE

right for me. I've worn them for fifteen years. Hiking boots are light and tough now, but I prefer these heavy ones. Our dog grows tense with happiness when I lace these boots, but not today. This is a desperation walk, and he senses a dark motive.

We begin. Our legs carry us and carry us. Just behind the house, perhaps a mile uphill, the trail begins, packed for us by a snowmobiler. We pass through mixed hardwood and small pine, then a beautiful section of young gray birch. The snow on the ground is clean, melted smooth. The birchbark is seamlessly beautiful, set on regular poles that go on as far as we can see. We come to old growth, white pines of perhaps a hundred years, a hundred feet tall, the favorite roosting rests of wild turkeys. We keep going.

The silence is so intense that we stop from time to time to listen to a branch scraping on another branch, a woodpecker drumming deadwood, far down the hill a motor revving. We've progressed to the place I usually turn around. Here the trail goes straight up, a narrowing alley of green-black, ferny hemlock. We climb. There is nothing to think. Nothing to do but step and step. The trees shut behind me. I walk beside the trail, punching toeholds, ascending, trying to outwalk death. With each step, the baby on my back grows. She's bigger, surely heavier, so heavy I don't think that I can move—except I do move. Maybe this is some strange and painful test of motherhood, or just brute *macha*. Near the top, we finally rest on a moss-cushioned boulder.

In the shelter of my parka, she nurses for the last time for days, then takes a graham cracker. I share a sandwich with our dog, and together we smell the dusty piles of leaves glowing rust red through the melt. I think of snowmobilers going straight down, their brakes burning, flying off the side of the trail, wrapping their machines around these old trees. My life is like that—I don't stop myself from going into the feeling, the emotion that pulls like gravity. Surely there are gentler courses, switchbacks, but for some reason I can't bring myself to take them. I was close to my grandmother in a way different than I am to anyone else in the world. We knew how to fight. Her death comes at me straight on.

Death is the least civilized rite of passage. The way we handle it, even with our loved ones, our old ones, is often strange, kitsch- and cliché-ridden, shocking. It is as if every time we encounter death it is a new invention. Three quarters of us die in hospitals, usually with no family present. The other quarter kick off anywhere—in streets, on planes, in our kitchens, at our writing desks. My grandmother, who fought death with cleverness and consistency and lots of brewer's yeast, would rather have died in her own backyard than in a hospital bed. She would have preferred to go while looking into the brilliant cups of her prize eight-foot-high hollyhocks, with a dog at her feet, birds pecking the slabs of suet she nailed to the bark of an old box elder by the door. A butcher's wife, she slit the necks of chickens for a living, gutted lambs, pulverized and sawed cows into steaks—and yet, she also loved animals.

My grandmother swore fierce and long in the butcher shop, and when I stayed with her, during my Catholic school years, I excused myself into the mulberry trees behind the slaughterhouse and prayed for her soul, fervently, until I heard her call me from the screen door to my cousinly task—cleaning gizzards.

After my uncle stuck his ice pick through each chicken's neck and, with razor knife and hands like big red cold scoops, gutted the chickens, filling coffee cans with gizzards, the task of any child who wanted supper was to turn the gizzards inside out and wash the tough little iridescent pouches clean of gravel.

Mary Erdrich Korll had lost her mother young and was raised by her father, a rough man. She adopted my father and his three brothers just before the Second World War, and she never developed a maternal voice around children, but treated them as equals and fixed upon us a fascinated eye. She had supported herself by writing newspaper jokes, wrapping butter, working as a telephone operator and in a traveling circus show. Running a butcher shop, ordering around grown men, taking care of several children at once, might have daunted anyone, but she seemed fearless to me and I felt in her a bracing lack of sweetness and a stringent honesty that lasted between us into adulthood. She was everybody's worthy adversary. Combative, sensual, aroused to protective furies, she was attentive to me as a person. She was my witness.

Now, looking down at the flowerless crowns of Eastern white pines, I remember the only old-growth trees I ever saw as a child, a grove in Little Falls, Minnesota, where I was born. The last time I visited my grandmother there, we went looking at those pines again, those sad giant remnants. Pens for wolves had been constructed among them. The sight of the caged wolves, one black, three gray, stopped my tongue. In the distance a train wailed and the wolves answered, tossing high their muzzles in speech that froze meaning.

My grandmother reached toward the wolves muttering as she would to a dog. Her eyes were cat-yellow. The implications of the moment were lost to her because she saw the wolves as simply there, existing, not tragic or much more beautiful or interesting than anything else. She put her hands through the wires to pet them and when they didn't move close, just stood in their own power and evaded her stare, she shrugged, drew her hand back. She had in her pockets a couple of pounds of homemade dog biscuits. Tossing them over the fence she called out, resignedly, to the whole pack, "All right, be that way!"

Hypothetical Pierogies

THEY WERE THE BEST THING SHE EVER MADE, the dish she was known for, the food of the gods, the manna, the festive occasion's one missing element. I hunger for these pierogies with a human hunger for the unattainable, for it is true that although she was famous for her pierogies, my grandmother made them only once.

I was eight years old, attaining the age of reason, subject to wrathful appetites. I encountered melting dough, smoky onions, sour cheese filling, edges browned in lard. Rotund pierogies filled me with a desire that would never be gratified. Understand, I had five younger siblings by then and even more cousins. We got only one, or two if we were extraordinarily quick. Ever after, it was the test of an occasion with my grandmother: Did it warrant pierogies? No, not quite, almost yes, not ever, actually. Maybe next time. Then no more.

So it was a mark of Michael's courage that he attempted the impossible—to replicate a childhood taste. Early on in our marriage he began to study the primal recipe, seriously, as one does the great problems in life. Using experts and books to approach the conundrum, Michael grappled with the Great Perfection. The first time he made pierogies, however, on a visit from my parents, astounding publishing news intervened just as he had pinched each pouch together. He stored them in the refrigerator as best he could and drove to town in a storm of excitement.

When we returned, the pierogies had merged, amoebalike, and were indivisible—one doughy mass.

Occasions came, occasions went, and always, strangely, there was some peculiar reason that Michael's pierogies failed. In the middle of making one batch, our well went dry, condemning us to those TV dinners. He scorched the onions another time, celebrating a first tooth. He offered to make pierogies for my grandmother on a legendary visit, but she declined and asked for honey-ginger chicken wings instead. I made them. They were passable. But afterward, her plate a mass of tiny picked bones—only the Polish and the Ojibwa clean bones so well—she looked at me fiercely and declared her allegiance to pierogies. She voiced her disdain for wings with a scornful phrase that struck into my ego like an arrow's shaft.

I wouldn't give you five cents for a truckload!

So naturally, now, a sense of taking one's fate in hand surrounds the making of pierogies. It is a tempting of the Powers. And still, because Michael is a man who never gives up on anything, a man who will risk all for a piece of stuffed dough, perhaps because he jousts with destiny on a regular basis in fiction, he tries again and again to make the pierogies.

They turn out nicely, but never quite perfectly because ... well—the water comes too hot from the tap, the filling is not up to par, a delicate phone call intervenes. They are still not quite the paragon dish whose secrets died locked in the person of my grandmother. Not quite. Not yet.

PIEROGIES
Makes about 4 dozen

Dough
1 package dry yeast
1 teaspoon honey
1 cup lukewarm water
1 ½ cups whole wheat flour
1 ½ cups unbleached all-purpose flour
⅓ cup vegetable oil
2 pinches salt

Mushroom Filling
1 cup finely chopped onion or shallots
2 garlic cloves, minced
2 tablespoons vegetable oil
½ ounce dried shiitake or porcini mushrooms,
    soaked until soft

1 cup finely chopped fresh mushrooms
3 ounces softened cream cheese, or mashed
  potatoes
½ cup chopped scallions
1 teaspoon dill weed
½ teaspoon black pepper
Salt to taste
2 slices dark slightly stale bread (rye or
  pumpernickel)
1 cup cottage cheese, or ½ cup sour cream
3 hard-boiled eggs, finely chopped
1 egg yolk, beaten with 1 tablespoon water
Poppy seeds, for sprinkling

1. *To make the dough:* Dissolve the yeast and honey in the water and let sit in a warm place for 10 minutes.

2. Combine the flours. Mix the oil, salt, and 2 cups of the flour into the dissolved yeast. Stir until smooth, then lit sit for half an hour.

3. Mix in remaining flour, then knead on floured board until dough is elastic and not sticky.

4. Place in a lightly oiled bowl, turning once to coat top. Cover with wax paper and place in a warm spot until doubled in size (about 1½ hours).

5. *To begin the filling:* Sauté onions and garlic in oil until soft.

6. Drain soaked mushrooms on a paper towel, then chop coarsely and mix with fresh mushrooms. Add to pan, continue to sauté, covered, about 5 minutes.

7. Remove from heat and mix with cream cheese (or cold mashed potatoes). Add scallions, dill, pepper, and salt to taste. Stir thoroughly. Crumble the bread into the mixture, then add cottage cheese and chopped eggs.

8. Preheat oven to 375 degrees.

9. Punch down the dough and refrigerate until ready to use. Pull off one piece of dough at a time, about the size of a walnut and shape into a ball. Roll it lightly in cornstarch and place between two sheets of wax paper. Roll lightly with a rolling pin into a square. Remove from wax paper and add about ½ teaspoon of the filling.

10. Moisten the edge of the dough with water and fold over. Press with the tines of a fork to seal. Place on an ungreased cookie sheet. Continue until all dough is used up.

11. Brush the tops with the egg yolk mixture and sprinkle with poppy seeds. Bake 20 minutes or until golden on top and done on the bottom—or, for even more calories and more delicious pierogies, deep-fry for about 4 minutes in a wire basket in vegetable oil (heated to 375 degrees), turning often with slotted spoon. Drain on paper towels.

SALMON PIROG
Makes 1 large pirog; serves 10 to 12

Michael learned to make this pirog, or pierogi, in Alaska. It makes a very substantial main course and should be served with no more than a light, tossed salad.

1 package dry yeast
¼ cup lukewarm water
¼ pound butter
1 cup scalded milk
1 teaspoon salt
2 teaspoons sugar
4 ½ to 5 cups flour
3 eggs, lightly beaten
4 cups cooked and chilled white rice
Salmon Filling (recipe follows)
6 hard-boiled eggs, chopped

1 egg yolk, lightly beaten with 2 tablespoons
   water
Dill (for garnish)

1. In a large bowl, dissolve the yeast in the luke-warm water. Melt the butter into the milk. Add the salt and sugar to the milk and cool to lukewarm. Add the milk mixture to the yeast mixture.

2. Beat in 1 cup of the flour. Beat in the eggs and then gradually beat in enough additional flour to make a soft dough. Turn the dough out on a lightly floured board and knead until soft and elastic.

3. Place in a lightly greased bowl, turning once to grease top. Cover with wax paper and place in a warm spot for 2 hours, or until the dough has doubled in bulk.

4. Preheat oven to 400 degrees.

5. Roll out the dough on a lightly floured pastry cloth in a rectangle (about 18 x 14 inches).

6. Spread a layer of rice in the middle of the prepared dough, then a layer of the salmon mixture to cover it, then a layer of the chopped hard-boiled eggs. The filling should be shaped like a meat loaf in the center of the dough, leaving at least 4 inches all around. Repeat several times, but finish with a layer of rice.

7. Draw the long edge of the dough together over the filling and—dipping your finger in water, if necessary—pinch to seal. Cut off a triangle from each corner, then fold remaining triangle ends like envelope flaps over the covered filling, and seal.

8. Place a lightly greased and floured baking sheet face down on the sealed edges. Holding the pastry cloth firmly, turn the cloth, filled roll, and pan over, all together, so that the smooth dough is uppermost.

9. Brush pirog with the egg yolk mixture. Make 4 steam holes in the top in a row along the center. Bake the pirog for 15 to 20 minutes or until golden. Reduce heat to 350 degrees and cook for 15 minutes more, until bottom is firm. Decorate with dill snips.

SALMON FILLING

½ cup finely chopped shallots
1 garlic clove, minced
4 tablespoons butter
¾ pound mushrooms, sliced

2 tablespoons dill
½ cup fish stock
½ teaspoon salt
¼ teaspoon white pepper
Dash of grated nutmeg
4 salmon steaks, poached, cooled, and flaked,
    with skin and bones removed, or 2 large cans
    of salmon, picked over

1. Sauté the shallots and garlic in the butter until tender. Add mushrooms and dill and cook 3 to 5 minutes over medium heat, stirring frequently.

2. Add stock, salt, pepper, and nutmeg and bring to a boil. Cook until excess liquid has evaporated, about 10 to 12 minutes.

3. Remove pan from stove. Mix in the salmon and cool to lukewarm.

Mourning Cloaks

A HOUSE IN THE WOODS IS SUBJECT TO small and persistent invasions from the outside. It is not just a human shelter, but a place offering congenial habitats to all sorts of other species. After returning from the second funeral, upon opening the house, after setting my pens out and brewing a cup of tea, I find that in my absence caterpillars have moved in everywhere, attached themselves to ceiling, walls, the edges of doors, fixed themselves with a sort of Superglue, and woven themselves into small gray lumpy cocoons.

Last year, the same caterpillars entered and built their nests, and now I know exactly what will happen to them. They are ugly little things, and I was certain that from them something equally unattractive would emerge—plain brown moths perhaps, or at best, a couple of cabbage butterflies.

But now I know. One morning when the weather turns warm, I will walk into the room and discover that from each one a tiny scrap of black velvet is beginning to break. Picturing a house of moths, beating themselves dead against the walls, I will find a box of tacks and carefully, without disturbing the small nascent being, chisel each trembling cocoon free with a spoon and tack it by the very tip, the glue end, to the lattice just outside my door.

Mourning Cloaks.

The name comes to me while I am thinking of my grandmother's tough-eyed stare, the twist of her mouth when she laughed, the henna red she dyed her hair. Watching each butterfly emerge, I will let go of a memory, a thought, of the old voices, of the connections beyond this time, winding into the past. All day, the butterflies will draw their wet, folded wings from the papery husks. They are discreet, buff and brown, trimmed with a rich dark stripe. Five, ten, twenty Mourning Cloaks, so many I can't count, will fan and vibrate. They cling to the blue-gray lattice of the porch in the coming spring, they dry and stiffen their wings, before they launch into the yard.

Weaning

OUR BABY IS ALMOST A YEAR OLD, AND down to one or two breast-feedings a day. If we miss one, she begins to suck my collar cuffs, makes cloth nipples between her fists and wet marks on my shirt. I soothe myself with her need, too, for I hate to wean her. Time stops around us for a moment, scenes held in a snowy globe. Hold back! Stop! I panic, unprepared for change, but it's too late. She sweeps on in her life. I cannot gather back one moment, only marvel at what comes next.

There was a time when each of our children gained enough weight so they couldn't possibly be fit inside of me again. I breathed out in relief, regret. As though they were foldable, like paper origami swans! Letting them go also is a process of bending the bow. Fortunately, consolations are built into every stage of a baby's development, for with the loss of each infant trait a new and fascinating talent of being emerges. She forgets to nurse primarily because she wants to *talk* to me. I can see it, looking into her eyes. She forgets her hunger and the old comfort pales because she wants to tell me something and to hear her own voice in her ears. She begins to loop sounds into long complicated vowels that hold meaning. Words get her things. She knows it. She has power over her desire. In a wholly new way I thrill at seeing her take charge of what she wants. Cracker. Ball. *Do-dush-abo*, meaning "breast-water," the Ojibwa word for milk.

Leap Day

As I WRITE THIS, MY LEFT HAND RESTS lightly on baby's back. She's trying to sleep but doesn't want me to put her down. With two fingers, I stroke the hair above her aching ear. If I take the fingers away, she wakes, she wails, as if my hand served a medicinal purpose. My arm below the elbow feels enormous, throbs with blood, seems almost to hum with electricity. It's a toss-up which will first loose consciousness: my arm or her head. At her inoculation last week, our-four-year-old shrieked in surprise at the sudden pain of the needle. Then, to take the hurt away, she put the sting against my bare arm, held our skin together. Her tears stopped. My flesh still had magic. I could absorb her pain by touch.

The Baby-sitter

AS OUR BABY GROWS MORE INTO HER OWN life, so I recover mine, but it is an ambiguous blessing. With one hand I drag the pen across the page and with the other, the other hand, I cannot let go of hers. There comes a day when we're at odds. I look at her, she looks at me. I put her down in a playpen filled with toys but she wants me and me alone after five minutes. I take her from the playpen, hold her, but she's not a lap baby for long anymore and wants to move, move anywhere. Soon she is bumping, creeping, undulating, standing, making her way through the little house on a hazardous obstacle course of delight.

There is a time in a baby's life when parents practically live at a crouch. She wants to move no matter what, to engage with the world. She is not a sleeper, but naps in short drops and then is ready for the adventure of me. I've just begun a thought, I'm writing my way in, when she laughs herself awake and bolts up, expectant, her grin wide, her eyes wild and magnetic, an electricity of hope rising off her, a thrill of mirth.

Her smile is so touching, so alight. I put my head down on my desk and within the dark cave of my hands a shout gathers. I'm at the moment. I will turn to her and lay aside this story, but with loss. I will play with her but part of me won't be there. Conflict has entered our perfect circle in a new set of clothes, and I'm torn between wanting to be with her always and needing to be—through writing and through concentration—who I am.

How perfectly, how generously she fits into my arms, how comfortably I receive her. How unsurpassed and fine. She props herself up on a chair and roams it, standing and dragging herself around its edges, nearly pulling it over onto herself. She dives for the woodstove tongs. I lunge after her, remove them. She creeps for the light socket. I divert her. She tries eagerly to stuff carpet lint, shoelaces, marbles, cat food, dustpan, bark, paper clip, fork, ancient noodle, the cat herself, gravel, shoe, mop board, book, toy into her mouth. I remove these things from her spit damp fists. She makes for me, won't let me hold her. Goes hell-bent for the bathroom where she once found a toilet pond. She goes after table legs with teeth, puts her hands under rockers, grabs, clutches, falls, screams, goes blue, comes up laughing in my arms.

When she's had enough and I can nurse her, when she's tense with eager hunger in my arms and then quieter, quieter, regrouping for her next set of bold charges and forays, when at last I can hold her for a space of time, I finally talk. I finally tell her I need help.

THE FIRST HALF day with the baby-sitter is a misery. Jean is a kind and forthright woman licensed for day care in her home. A small mother with dark eyes and a sweet smile, a woman who has been caring for babies for many years, even Jean is surprised by how long our baby manages to cry. Scream. Wail. Fret. I know the water torture and I hope Jean can wait it out. One hour. Another half. Two. My breasts burn, blood pumps hard in my temples. I call. Behind Jean's voice our baby's roar, continual and harsh as the sea, breaks and falls, over and over.

I get into the car and pick baby up. The experiment is not repeated for a short while—then, then, the change. A hard week of teething, the first sudden breakthrough in language, and we try again. Little by little, she looks forward to this new routine. It happens. One day a week, two, finally three, she grows more out of my life and into her own.

The hours stretch wide on the mornings I work alone. Time expands in a blue haze. I am lighter, fuller, ballooning with stunned surprise. I constantly possess the feeling we usually have only momentarily, the where-was-I that causes us to slap at our foreheads. I'm trying to jostle out the thoughts. *Where was I? Where was I?* Of course, I know. I was in an ambiguous heaven, a paradise both difficult and temporary, the only kind on earth we know.

I ease into the day making noise, banging the tea kettle, rich in my aloneness again. Outside, the hoarfrost glitters, chickadees flip through the air, the weeds and the branches of the trees are outlined with a fine brilliance. I am ready now to finish this book of scraps, of jottings, of notes and devotions taken at another time, another era in our lives. The little cat reclaims my lap and curls possessively beneath my hands, as I begin.

Francis for the last time

HE'S SLIGHTLY DRUNK, OFF BALANCE IN HIS movements, and very thin, but lucid and far-seeing, as though he's been to the top of a mountain. There he is at the edge of the yard, calmly waiting until I put out the milk-soaked cat food. He approaches, crouches ceremoniously, chews with one side of his jaw. Perhaps he has been nicked by a car and suffered nerve damage, perhaps he's ill. He will not be caught, not even approach the live trap's wire entrance, so the best I can do is feed him and pretend he isn't living in the hay bales and bundled blankets against the side of the house.

Working alone on a baby-sitter day, I hear a strange sound, a dream sound, an odd lisping voice like a little person in a folk tale calling, *Hewp! Hewp!*

Hewp! It is the most piteous cry, so full of agitated misery that I rush to the door too quickly to wonder what I'll find. I burst out and look around frantically—nothing. But still the humanlike call. *Hewp!* I whirl, and see that Francis has caught—no, *tackled*—a large buff-colored rabbit. This is not a wild rabbit, but somebody's pet gone loose, as is Francis. The rabbit is a lovely creature with magnificent fur and lovely, rich, dark eyes. Francis is fixed in his intent, holding on to the rabbit but losing purchase because his claws have apparently dulled. As for his teeth, there's the problem. He's lost them. The rabbit's safe, just pinned down, wrestled to a terrified halt, and still calling, bleating. Francis is so intent on his prey that he doesn't remember for a moment that he's a feral beast. I unclench his paws, drag him away. The rabbit bounds into the yard. Francis trembles, all toothless appetite. I let him go. He slowly walks into the trees.

Dream

ONE DAY, ONE NIGHT, I'LL DREAM A DREAM, perhaps like any other dream, except that I won't know it is the last dream of my life.

❊　　❊　　❊

I AM keeping track for baby, waiting for her to
dream something that she can put into words. There
are spaces on the baby calendar for the first tooth, the
first smile, the first word, but nowhere to record the
first dream. I leave space in the margins and wait. She
has been dreaming all along, there is no question
watching her face complex in sleep, her eyes moving
under delicate, violet-pink, sunrise lids.

Grand elk moving underneath the grand sky.
Tyrant blue jays. Cats loping bannerlike across the
fields. Moths fanning their pale wings against the
light. Spiders. Brown recluse, marked like a violin.
The beating of a heart perhaps, moving in, moving
out. My own voice—perhaps she dreams my own
voice as I dream hers—starting out of sleep, awake,
certain that she's cried out.

For years now I have been dreaming the powerful anxiety dreams of all parents. Something is lost,
something must be protected. A baby swims in an
aquarium, a baby sleeps in a suitcase. The suitcase
goes astray, the airline company will not return it. I
spend all night arguing with people at a baggage
claims desk. Parents endure exhausting nights
searching drawers and running through corridors and

town streets and emptying laundry baskets looking for their missing babies. Mine is hiding in a washing machine or behind a Corinthian column or out in the long grass, the endless grass. Mine is running toward the nameless sky.

Now, as I move into the pages of manuscripts, I fall asleep anxious but embark on no tiring searches through piles of bricks and train stations. The dream junk and dream treasure, the excess bliss and paranoia, goes into the pages of books. I do not dream when I am writing.

Walking

TO PULL HERSELF UPRIGHT, TO STRAIN upward, to climb, has been baby's obsession for the past three months and now, on her first birthday, it is that urge I celebrate and fear. She has pulled herself erect by the strings of her sister's hair, by using my clothes, hands, earrings, by the edges and the rungs and the unstable handles of the world. She has yanked herself up, stepped, and it is clear from her grand excitement that walking is one of the most important things we ever do. It is raw power to go forward, to lunge, catching at important arms and hands, to take control of the body, tell it what to do, to leave behind the immobility of babyhood. With each step she swells, her breath goes ragged and her eyes darken in a shine of happiness. A glaze of physical joy covers her, moves through her, more intense than the banged forehead, bumped chin, the bruises and knocks and losses, even than the breathtaking falls and solid thumps, joy more powerful than good sense.

It would seem she has everything she could want—she is fed, she is carried, she is rocked, put to sleep. But no, *walking* is the thing, the consuming urge to seize control. She has to walk to gain entrance to the world. From now on, she will get from here to there more and more by her own effort. As she goes, she will notice worn grass, shops or snow or the shapes of trees. She will walk for reasons other than to get somewhere in particular. She'll walk to think or not to think, to leave the body, which is often the same as becoming at one with it. She will walk to ward off anger in its many forms. For pleasure, purpose, or to grieve. She'll walk until the world slows down, until her brain lets go of everything behind and until her eyes see only the next step. She'll walk until her feet hurt, her muscles tremble, until her eyes are numb with looking. She'll walk until her sense of balance is the one thing left and the rest of the world is balanced, too, and eventually, if we do the growing up right, she will walk away from us.